Wooden Spoon
The children's charity of rugby

RUGBYWORLD
Yearbook 2016

Editor
Ian Robertson

Photographs
Getty Images

Published in the UK in 2015 by
Lennard Publishing, an imprint of
Lennard Associates Ltd,
Mackerye End,
Harpenden, Herts AL5 5DR
email: orders@lennardqap.co.uk

Distributed by G2 Entertainment
c/o Orca Book Services
160 Eastern Avenue, Milton Park
Abingdon, OX14 4SB

ISBN: 978-1-78281-290-6

Production editor: Chris Marshall
Text and cover design: Paul Cooper

Caricature of Charlie Hodgson on page 91 by John Ireland

The publishers would like to thank Getty Images for providing most of the photographs for
this book. The publishers would also like to thank AIG, Fotosport UK, Fotosport Italy, Inpho
Photography, World Rugby, Chris Thau and Wooden Spoon for additional material.

Printed and bound in Italy
by L.E.G.O. S.p.A

Contents

We focus on the most important economy in the world. Yours.

Your personal economy is always with you. But it's only when we step back and look at all the different aspects of your life, that we are able to see yours. It shows how your family, your home, your passions and your career are all intertwined. We see how it's unique to you and constantly changing. So at HSBC Premier our focus is on providing personal support, for your personal economy.

Find out more at hsbcpremier.com/personaleconomy

HSBC Premier is subject to financial eligibility criteria.

HSBC ◆◆
Premier

FOREWORD

by HRH THE PRINCESS ROYAL

BUCKINGHAM PALACE

HRH The Princess Royal,
Royal Patron of Wooden Spoon.

As Royal Patron of the Wooden Spoon Society, the children's charity of rugby, I have visited many of the projects the charity supports and met the inspirational children and their families that benefit from its work. Since the charity was founded in 1983, Wooden Spoon has helped over a million disadvantaged and disabled children and their families in the UK and Ireland. It funds a range of projects which are not just rugby focused. It is one of the country's largest funders of respite and medical treatment centres, sensory rooms, specialist playgrounds, sports activity areas and community based programmes. Despite being a national charity, Wooden Spoon has over 400 committed volunteers raising money in local communities. A distinct characteristic of the charity is that funds are spent in the local area where they are raised.

Rugby has always defined Wooden Spoon. The charity's roots lie in rugby and its future is shaped by it. On the field, enthusiasm, integrity, teamwork and fun are foundations for all those involved in the game, and off the field, they provide the driving force for the charity. The game's culture inspires Wooden Spoon. With the continued support and commitment of leading sporting personalities through to clubs and local communities, rugby has provided all those involved with a purpose in making a positive difference for over 30 years.

2015 is an exciting year as England hosts the Rugby World Cup. Wooden Spoon is celebrating the many things that rugby has given to people who have played it, supported it and been supported through it. I encourage you to support Wooden Spoon to ensure that it continues to help change the lives of disadvantaged and disabled children living in your local community.

Anne

WE ARE RUGBY.

Wooden Spoon
The children's charity of rugby

Love rugby?
Get involved

Together we can change children's lives through the power of rugby.

visit the website to find out more:

wswearerugby.org.uk   #wearerugby

Craig's story

Wooden Spoon
The children's charity of rugby

When Craig* was asked to leave home at 16 by his mum, his life was heading in a downhill direction. Craig's mum felt unable to cope, as Craig drifted further into spending time on the streets, taking drugs and hanging around with a bad crowd.

Placed in a children's home, Craig was feeling stuck in life. He was desperate for independence but couldn't see a way of being able to support himself. He became more frustrated and bitter about his future.

Thankfully, just when things were looking very bleak for Craig, he found crucial support through a special Wooden Spoon funded project – HITZ.

With their help, Craig was given the support he needed to develop a focus and learn life skills in order to support himself. The programme enabled him to get involved in education again, learn employability skills and boost his mood and self-esteem through rugby.

Craig secured himself a job with the local council; he now lives in his own accommodation and has a great support network. He has even started rebuilding a relationship with his mum.

The money you raise can help many young people living in desperate situations turn their lives around, and in turn, make a positive impact on society.

The money you raise can help many young people living in desperate situations turn their lives around, and in turn, make a positive impact on society.

*Names and specific circumstances have been changed to protect the identity of the young person.

Let's TRY and use the power of rugby to change children's lives

Hello, my name is Phil Vickery.

I am lead ambassador for Wooden Spoon. I'm passionate about the charity because I really believe that rugby can change children's and young peoples lives, and I want you to help us do more.

This year is going to be one of the most exciting for rugby in the UK and Ireland, we are celebrating the many things that the sport has given to all the people who have played it, supported it and been helped through it. We are using this opportunity to launch our 'We Are Rugby' campaign.

From cooking for your mates, to organising a race night at work, to co-ordinating your own rugby tournament at school or college, we are asking you to raise money and help make an incredible difference to disadvantaged and disabled children's lives across the UK and Ireland.

I have had the privilege to visit many of the projects Wooden Spoon supports. Someone who really sticks in my mind is Maxine* who had tragically lost her son, Archie* to a life-limiting condition.

Despite everything she had been through, Maxine was so thankful to us as a charity. With the accommodation we funded at the children's hospice where Archie was cared for, Maxine and her family were able to spend his last days all together.

She was so appreciative that, with our help, she was with her child in his final stages of life. That's the kind of life-changing support we can make happen.

So you see it doesn't matter what you do as long as you do something. This handy fundraising pack will help you raise as much as you can, and every penny helps change even more lives.

Thank you for everything you're about to do.

You're brilliant.

Phil Vickery

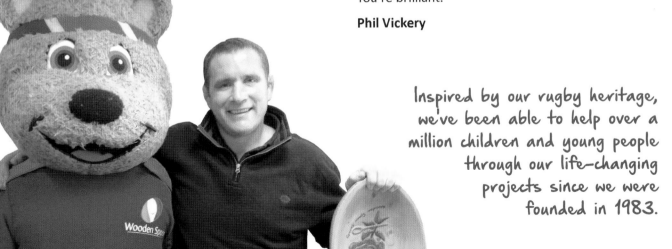

Inspired by our rugby heritage, we've been able to help over a million children and young people through our life-changing projects since we were founded in 1983.

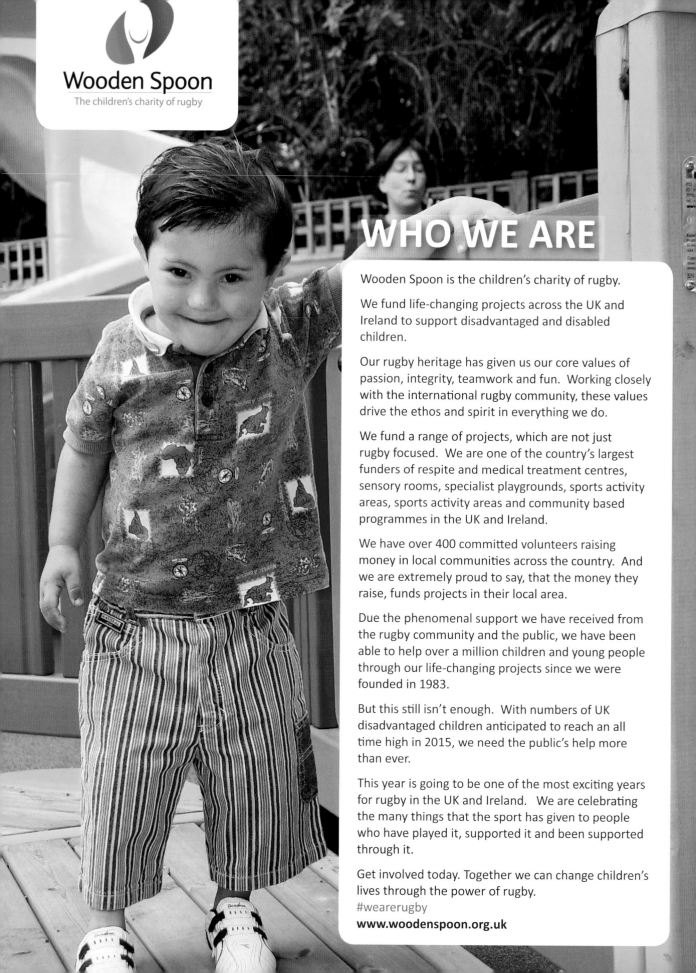

![Wooden Spoon — The children's charity of rugby]

WHO WE ARE

Wooden Spoon is the children's charity of rugby.

We fund life-changing projects across the UK and Ireland to support disadvantaged and disabled children.

Our rugby heritage has given us our core values of passion, integrity, teamwork and fun. Working closely with the international rugby community, these values drive the ethos and spirit in everything we do.

We fund a range of projects, which are not just rugby focused. We are one of the country's largest funders of respite and medical treatment centres, sensory rooms, specialist playgrounds, sports activity areas, sports activity areas and community based programmes in the UK and Ireland.

We have over 400 committed volunteers raising money in local communities across the country. And we are extremely proud to say, that the money they raise, funds projects in their local area.

Due the phenomenal support we have received from the rugby community and the public, we have been able to help over a million children and young people through our life-changing projects since we were founded in 1983.

But this still isn't enough. With numbers of UK disadvantaged children anticipated to reach an all time high in 2015, we need the public's help more than ever.

This year is going to be one of the most exciting years for rugby in the UK and Ireland. We are celebrating the many things that the sport has given to people who have played it, supported it and been supported through it.

Get involved today. Together we can change children's lives through the power of rugby.

#wearerugby

www.woodenspoon.org.uk

THE STORY BEHIND WOODEN SPOON

A wonderful legacy emerged in 1983 after five England rugby supporters went to Dublin to watch England in the final game of the Five Nations Championship against the Irish. The game was lost 25-15 and England finished last in the table with just a single point gained from their draw against Wales.

After the match, in a Dublin bar surrounded by celebrating Ireland supporters, the five England supporters sought some consolation only for three of their Irish friends to present them with a wooden spoon, wrapped in an Irish scarf on a silver platter as a memento of England's dismal season.

Accepting the gift with good humour and grace, the England fans resolved to hold a golf match to see who would have the honour of keeping the wooden spoon. Just a few months later the golf match was held and in the course of an entertaining day an astonishing sum of £8,450 was raised. The money was used to provide a new minibus for a local special needs school, Park School. This was to be the of first many Wooden Spoon charitable projects that has grown to over 600 in the years since.

From defeat on the rugby field, and a tongue-in-cheek consolation prize, the Wooden Spoon charity was born.

OUR ROYAL PATRON

Our Royal Patron is HRH The Princess Royal who gives generously of her time.

OUR RUGBY PATRONS

The IRFU, RFU, WRU, SRU, RFL all support us in our charitable work.

SPORTING PARTNERS

We work closely with a variety of clubs, league associations and governing bodies who help us achieve our vision of improving young lives though the power of rugby.

Buy a woolly hat!

Wooden Spoon
The children's charity of rugby

Chris Robshaw, Michael Owen, even Sir Ranulph Fiennes
are wearing our wonderful woolly hats!

Don't miss out on your limited edition Wooden Spoon woolly hat.
Buy online at **woodenspoon.org.uk/woollyhat**

Sir Ranulph Fiennes

Alex Cuthbert

Michael Owen

Every woolly hat raises much needed funds for
disabled and disadvantaged children and young
people across the UK and Ireland.

COMMENT & FEATURES

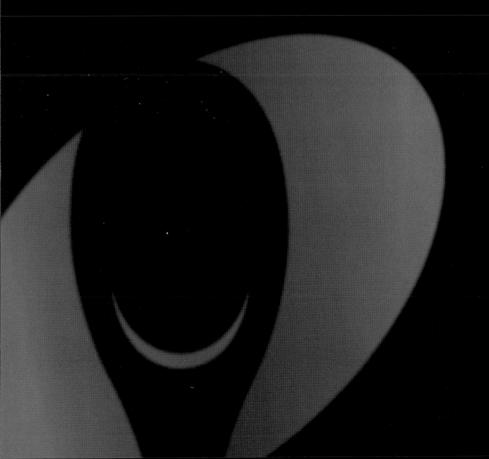

Making History
the All Blacks in Samoa

by CHRIS FOY

'It took an age to make the short journey to their hotel, as the whole route was lined by villagers who had waited into the night just to see the coach glide by'

The All Blacks who were there will never forget it – from the wild hysteria that greeted them to the big hits they had to endure on the field at Apia Park. New Zealand's first Test visit to Samoa was a unique career experience for those who took part. It was an unprecedented sensory onslaught for the players, coaches and support staff who flew from Auckland to the Pacific Island nation. For the whole duration of their stay, which lasted just three days, the world champions were met by an outpouring of affection and sheer, unrestrained joy from the locals who descended on the capital for any fleeting glimpse of their rugby idols. But Steve Hansen's men were also met by a runaway train on 8 July in the form of a fired-up Manu Samoa side, who made a mockery of the perceived gulf in class to push the All Blacks to the brink of a seismic upset.

This was an historic occasion which was long overdue. Despite close ties between the countries and a growing volume of two-way player traffic – with a long pattern of Samoans representing New Zealand offset more recently by Kiwis pledging allegiance to the Manu cause – the sport's premier Test nation had never come to town. Grumbles of protest about the imbalance in the relationship had become louder and more persistent. When Sir Graham Henry visited Samoa in 2012 with the Webb Ellis Cup, won by his All Blacks the previous year, he was urged to help bring his national team to Apia. A media campaign in New Zealand gathered momentum and in September 2014 the dam burst – the game was confirmed.

Having agreed to the fixture, the NZRU were urged to honour it in fitting fashion, and to their credit that is what they did. Despite Hansen being deprived of some 17 leading players who were involved in the all-Kiwi Super 15 final between the Highlanders and Hurricanes, the head coach selected the strongest available line-up. Crucially, the two veteran icons, captain Richie McCaw and Dan Carter, were both chosen to start.

The All Blacks gathered at Auckland airport in Polynesian-themed team shirts. They knew they would be well received, but nothing prepared them for the mayhem upon arrival. Tiny Faleolo

RIGHT Samoan fans greet Richie McCaw and Steve Hansen after the All Blacks paraded through Apia the day before the match.

airport outside Apia was heaving when the tourists landed at 10.30pm. Good-natured chaos ensued; with ceremonial war dances by the runway and in the cramped terminal building, followed by a cacophony of acclaim when the players ventured outside.

It took an age to make the short journey to their hotel, as the whole route was lined by villagers who had waited into the night just to see the coach glide by. What the darkness masked was that the entire island of Upolu was decked out for the event. There was coloured bunting everywhere, banners of support for both sides, thousands upon thousands of roadside painted coconuts, and effigies of players placed on patches of grass or even on boats moored by the coast road. In some cases, villages had mocked up entire rugby matches complete with posts and pitch markings.

Prior to leaving New Zealand, Hansen noted wryly that some aspects of the Test build-up would be 'a bit different'. He spoke of having to embrace the unusual aspects of the experience. Sure enough, the next day, when the All Blacks would typically have a short training session and then rest and finalise planning, they were required to take part in a parade through Apia, under the midday sun. While the Samoa players walked through the crowded streets, the visitors were driven along in ornate, old-fashioned, open-sided buses decorated with palm leaves and flowers. There were people watching their progress from every conceivable vantage point on pavements, in vehicles, on office roofs and balconies and leaning precariously out of windows. No wonder that many All Blacks saw fit to capture the scenes on mobile phones. It was a remarkable spectacle.

There was an official reception hosted by Samoa's prime minister, Tuilaepa Sailele Malielegaoi, during which McCaw demonstrated his elevation to the status of rugby statesman with a gracious, humorous speech. Yet, in the extreme heat, the tourists appeared uncomfortable at times. They wanted the next day to come, so they could get on with the game.

The danger was that a mismatch would have undermined the whole worthy exercise, but the lucky few who had tickets were treated to a gladiatorial encounter. The All Blacks seemed to have seized control when debutant George Moala touched down after half-time, but the sheer ferocity of the home defence unsettled them. In the 66th minute, Bath flanker Alafoti Faosiliva crashed over for a try and the conversion put the hosts back within a single score. Samoa launched a furious late onslaught, but New Zealand hung on to win 25-16. The result meant there was honour on both sides and the players mingled for a shared picture by the touch line after the final whistle, which illustrated the close bonds between them.

What followed was more good-natured chaos, as fans swarmed on to the field – taking advantage of the relaxed security – to request selfies and autographs. There was a tangible sense of goodwill, and McCaw and co., while bruised and battered, were visibly touched by the whole colourful circus. The festivities went on late into the night, in Apia and around the island of Upolu. The next day, before heading home, Hansen attended a ceremony in the village of Vaiala, where he was named an honorary high chief.

While the All Blacks departed with the gratitude of a small neighbouring nation, only time will tell if their historic match in Apia will serve as a watershed, or as a glorious one-off. In the immediate aftermath, Hansen and several players indicated their desire to return one day and that message appeared genuine, but the powers that be at their union and others are seemingly reluctant to send leading Test teams to the Pacific. The siren call to do so has grown louder still, but for all the outside pressure based on a desire to develop these tiny and remote hotbeds of the game, the bottom line is that the Tier One countries are slow to embrace fixtures which don't earn them money. Such small markets do not produce the desired revenue to make themselves appealing destinations, but the pressure on unions to put aside financial misgivings will continue to increase.

Sadly, the Samoa Rugby Union actually made a loss hosting the All Blacks, but regular high-profile matches at home would boost profits. And that is just part of the equation. There and in Fiji and Tonga, there is a craving to see the global powers at close quarters. These nations have surely earned that right – such has been their impact on the game far from their shores. It is staggering to note that in the entire history of the game, the three Pacific teams have hosted just 20 Tests against the eight leading countries in the world: Australia, New Zealand, South Africa, England, Ireland, Scotland, Wales and France. That is a shameful record of sustained neglect.

England are the richest rugby nation, yet they have played twice in Fiji – in 1988 and 1991, during the old amateur era – and have never ventured to Samoa or Tonga. There are no indications that they intend to consider following in New Zealand's footsteps. Lions years present the most obvious opportunity, but England have a recent tradition of heading to Argentina at such times. At least Wales have a Pacific tour planned for 2017, having last faced each of the three island sides away from home in 1994.

Granted, conditions can be testing at times. High temperatures and humidity are a factor in some cases, training facilities are limited in comparison with those of the wealthier nations and top-end hotels are less prevalent. There is also the logistical challenge of taking huge touring parties to distant places that require at least three flights in each direction – certainly from Europe. But that should not detract from the bigger picture, of doing what is right for the greater good of the game. Fijians, Samoans and Tongans are now an established part of the fabric of the game worldwide. They provide some of the most eye-catching flair and thunderous collisions that rugby is renowned for.

When England's players knelt on the Twickenham turf to join their Samoan counterparts in a post-match prayer in November 2014, it was a moving gesture of solidarity with club team-mates and rivals who were in dispute with their union. But the ultimate gesture would be for the touching act to be repeated one day, in Apia.

Your retirement *nest egg* could become a source of income PROFITS.

Now that the pension rules are changing, there are more ways to feather your retirement nest. With income funds, for example. And no-one knows more about income territory than the Artemis hunters. We have expert Profit hunters in Strategic Bonds, Income, Global Income and Monthly Distribution. Each offering a compelling alternative to putting all of your nest egg into one annuity basket. Please remember that past performance should

Fig. 1:
A typical
PROFIT

not be seen as a guide to future performance. The value of an investment and any income from it can fall as well as rise as a result of market and currency fluctuations and you may not get back the amount originally invested.

PORTFOLIO ADVISER
WINNER
Readers' choice
FUND AWARDS 2015

ARTEMIS
The PROFIT Hunter

0800 092 2051   *investorsupport@artemisfunds.com*   *artemis.co.uk*

Men in the Middle
Refereeing the Modern Game

by TERRY COOPER

'To keep their standards the Premiership referees come to Twickenham on Mondays for a physical session in the morning and afternoon'

Have you ever wondered why the referee is often the second man to arrive when a long-range, breakaway try is dotted down: first the gallant defender, then the sprinting chap in a sponsor's shirt with a whistle?

Yes, they can run, these game-makers, decision-takers, game-breakers. That's because they have become as professional, as full-time, as the coaches and players, whose destiny they influence.

Tony Spreadbury, who used to ref with a smile on his face, even in Tests, and is now the Rugby Football Union's Head of Professional Game Match Officials, reveals a testing physical regime.

> **ABOVE** Refereeing with a smile on his face. Tony Spreadbury, now Head of Professional Game Match Officials at the RFU, in charge of the Powergen Cup quarter-final between Harlequins and Leicester at the Stoop in January 2002.

'We run farther than any player during a match. If we're there as
one of the first to arrive at a breakdown to make a decision the teams
don't argue, but if you're five metres behind, they'll query your call. To
keep their standards the Premiership referees come to Twickenham on
Mondays for a physical session in the morning and afternoon, then
Tuesdays include a three-hour session. During that start-the-week
gathering we have sports science coaches and there are fitness tests
every six weeks. In between these workouts we review all six weekend
matches from our point of view. One ref may have had a "train crash"
of a match and that can happen to any of us. We work on the
consistency that we want to bring to the Premiership and the
worldwide game. I refer to the Premiership referees as the thirteenth
team in the league.'

'Spreaders', as the players affectionately know him, and the ex-
referees who work with him at Twickenham, is on top of all the
niggling areas that irritate all you spectators.

Video verdicts: 'Going upstairs to the TMO was taking too long. Last
season we improved because referees are taking ownership on the
pitch of the decision by looking at the screens, which are now on every
Premiership ground. That enhances on-field discipline. The ref is the
most experienced person. But he was asking the less experienced
bloke upstairs to make the call. The TMO is used more now when an HD screen is necessary.'

Refs coaching players, as in 'Leave it, Blue 7': He admits to a change of heart. 'I talked for England
during a game. Now I think: less is best. For instance, teams were not rolling away when told until
the second shout and the damage had been done. Now the chatting is done in down time, when
there is a stoppage.'

Players trying to run the game: 'Huge characters from my time, like Matt Dawson and Lawrence
Dallaglio, must still be part of the game. But we can't allow them to take charge. I remember
Lawrence asking for a Gloucester man to get a card. I told him, "If you want cards, go to WH Smith."
And I used to tell all those who badgered me, "If you're shouting at me I can't concentrate on my

decisions." Down time is when they can raise issues and build a relationship. When Lawrence and Matt had retired and I went to Wasps I thought I had gone deaf it was so quiet at the back of their scrum.'

Addressing players by their Christian names: 'Captains only. You can't know all 30 first names. A quiet, informal word asking him by name to help keep the game going before we start getting formal.'

Offside when there is so much kick-chase: 'We've worked really hard, but it's difficult. The players have adapted by knowing the law. We go into the clubs to help them. We have to get the assistant referees to help, but it must be the wow factor as in "Wow, he's a mile offside".'

Reset scrums: 'We work with Graham Rowntree on the technical problems. We could resolve resets by telling the ref to penalise straightaway, but we need the right decision and sometimes it's not clear who took the scrum down. We don't want to remove a reset from the ref's armoury. Ultimately it's a pushing competition and we want to reward the dominant scrum, provided it's legal.'

Pity that Rowntree and other retired forwards can't realistically become refs. ('They couldn't keep up,' says Spreaders frankly.) But everybody knew that rugby had really entered the 21st century when former lock Wade Dooley was made a citing commissioner. Yes, Wade, England's enforcer from the 1980s and 1990s.

Unions worldwide believe they are getting rugby right, but the laws need plenty of tinkering. Spreaders discloses: 'Earlier this year World Rugby [the old International Board] met and there were 94 suggestions for potential law changes. They got rid of half of them, but the remainder will be looked at for possible small changes at the start of the next four-year cycle between World Cups.'

And when one of Spreaders' successors reluctantly shows a red card, what next for the offender? Many remember the old days, when a man's being sent off made him automatically guilty, and the only hope of emerging with a result was a verdict of 'Sending Off Sufficient' from a local panel

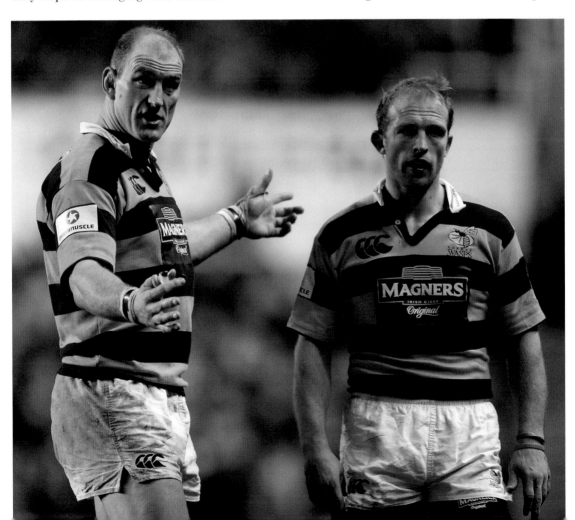

anticipating attacking their first G&T. 'Not guilty, old boy? Don't understand the meaning of the phrase.'

Many years back the unions recognised the need for a fair hearing leading to simple justice. The regulations relating to discipline comprise a massive, but necessary, 55 pages in the *RFU Handbook*. Everybody knows where they stand.

Gerard McEvilly, the RFU Head of Discipline since 2012, says: 'I deal with a variety of issues including case management and ensuring that cases are prepared for disciplinary and appeal panels. The process has moved on significantly. You still have situations where a player appears before an internal club panel and then the RFU or the County will deal with him formally and either ratify the decision or decide to apply a different sanction.

'At Level 5 and below we delegate powers to the Counties. We look after Levels 1 to 4, plus any appeals that come in from the Counties.

'At Levels 1 to 4 players appear before an RFU panel. We must have proper, regulatory formality because we are talking about suspending players who are professional or semi-professional and there have to be proper, defined processes, though we try not to operate it like a court structure. It's still a sports tribunal and does not have the same formality as a court. We must never move away from that.

'We are dealing with players of member clubs of the Union. And players may suffer financially as a result of being suspended.'

The disciplinarians have to be alert to trends in foul play.

'Where there seems to be a particular type of offence occurring across the Game we try to identify that and ensure that referees and Citing Commissioners are aware of these and deal with them properly.

'A few years ago it was the tip-tackle, where players were brought down on their head and shoulders and there was a risk of significant injury. The "entry point" [meaning the starting sanction related to the seriousness of the foul play] was increased. Recently we have had players being taken out in the air.

'Current offences on our radar include the chop-tackle where players roll or throw their bodies into an opponent's legs/knee area without any proper attempt to make a tackle, not using arms and potentially taking the knee against the joint.

'Then there is the crocodile roll whereby opponents are rolled out of mauls by grabbing their head. They are quite good at apt descriptions so that you understand what they're talking about. Dangerous clearing-out at the ruck and dangerous charging are others we ask referees and our 19 Citing Commissioners to keep an eye on.

'At the end of the season World Rugby highlighted the choke-hold, when the ball carrier is held above the shoulders.'

What about the tap-tackle? No arms there. Ed Morrison, England's only World Cup-final referee, once admitted, 'I don't know,' when asked why it was still legal, despite breaking all the definitions of a legitimate tackle. 'I agree with Ed,' said McEvilly. 'They have existed since we all played. But people accept that it's part of the game.' Nice to know that rugby still retains some of the 'Well, we've always done it like this, old chap' style.

McEvilly is a barrister and says: 'It is certainly helpful to have a legal background in the role given the variety of regulatory type cases that we deal with.

'I am often asked why a player got a two-week suspension and another four for the same offence. I say get hold of the relevant judgment from the RFU website. They are all published. There may be various reasons set out, for example a punch might have caused more significant injury, a player may have a more significant disciplinary record, another may have pleaded guilty, shown contrition etc. There are many different factors to look at, but mainly why the panel arrived at the entry point that it did for the offending. All players have the right to appeal if they feel the first panel erred in any way.'

next

ARE HAPPY TO SUPPORT THE

THE WOODEN SPOON

A Matter of Policy
the Overseas Player Ruling

by MICK CLEARY

'The Australian approach is to allow a partial loosening of the restrictions, with only players with 60 Wallaby caps or more eligible for dispensation'

What's wrong with playing rugby overseas? Playing in France did Rob Andrew no harm. Jonny Wilkinson certainly flourished there, too – fit, healthy, vibrant, alive, a far cry from the injury-blighted, angst-ridden individual who suffered far more than he prospered in the wake of the Sydney night of glory in 2003. There are others, too, who have found form as well as solace in foreign climes – Wallaby playmaker Matt Giteau at Toulon, Canadian lock Jamie Cudmore at Clermont, Pumas Juan Martín Fernández Lobbe and Patricio Albacete; the list is lengthy and distinguished. And the Armitage brothers at Toulon, Delon and Steffon? Big assets for their adopted club. So, too, former Bath full back Nick Abendanon at Clermont Auvergne, the 2015 European Player of the Year, following on from one Steffon Armitage. The roll-call is important. For in almost every case, the venture overseas has not been rugby's equivalent of a gap year, a chance for some fun in the sun, kick-back time, a break from the rigours of the domestic circuit, an easy-money gig. No, it is none of these things. In fact, it is quite the opposite. Nearly every player of note who has opted to ply his trade abroad has become a better player, not a paler imitation of his former self, a faded presence on the scene. There are exceptions – the Welsh contingent, for example, the Dan Lydiates, do not seem to

RIGHT Delon Armitage (with ball) and Steffon Armitage in action for Toulon in the 2014 Top 14 final. The RFU's selection policy regards players plying their trade overseas as ineligible for England except in 'exceptional circumstances'.

travel well, and even Ireland's Johnny Sexton struggled to fit in and make his mark at Racing Métro in Paris – but the overriding impression is that the foreign experience is a positive one. Players are better for the trip, more rounded, more grounded, more productive.

Why then does the RFU seek to exclude them from their plans? Not just for the 2015 Rugby World Cup, but for the foreseeable future. The door is well and truly shut. No Armitages. No Abendanon. No David Strettle, who forsook a place in the 2015 World Cup squad to take up a three-year contract with Clermont. And there will be no Manu Tuilagi, either, if he were to move to Toulouse as has been mooted, where he will join up with another England exile, Toby Flood. All gone – and as far as their international reckoning is concerned, discarded.

The English state of affairs is in sharp contrast to that of South Africa and Australia, leading powers in the global game yet who seem to have little difficulty with the notion that some of their best players may wish to play overseas, be it in France or Japan where there are far more riches on offer than in their homeland. The Wallabies have only recently felt minded to move their goalposts, lifting the self-same exclusion zone that the RFU has chosen to erect to allow players such as Giteau or Drew Mitchell to return to the international fold. The Australian approach is to allow a partial loosening of the restrictions, with only players with 60 Wallaby caps or more eligible for dispensation.

South Africa have no such qualms. Bryan Habana, Ruan Pienaar, Schalk Brits – just three of their number who have played for the Springboks in recent times. Bakkies Botha, Victor Matfield, Jaque Fourie, Fourie du Preez – these are major items in terms of their playing prowess. Yet South Africa have recognised the socio-economic realities of the professional game. The rand cannot compete in the currency market, certainly not when set against the all-powerful euro. The South African union has come to terms with that, and has given its blessing for its players to head overseas. And why

wouldn't those players look to maximise the value of their talent? Their careers could come to an end at any moment. One bad injury, and that could be it. A projected 12-year career reduced to a few years by one ferocious and unexpected contact.

The South African union was aware that several players would feel obliged to cash in on their worth while deals were on the table, particularly the older ones. Why should they be penalised for being good? So ran the argument. And the SA union accepted the realpolitik of the time. There is a downside, primarily that of player welfare and the danger of burn-out. Players are obliged to be available under World Rugby regulations on release for international windows, but what sort of state might a top-line player be in after a nine-months shift for a Top 14 paymaster? The Rugby Championship plays through the summer months of the northern hemisphere year, with those self-same Test stars expected to clock back on for duty with their respective clubs as soon as those international commitments are met. It is a brutal schedule, and not ideal for either party. The Argentine players face the same difficulties and the Argentine union is trying to come up with a package to attract their best players back home in order to be able to resource a Super Rugby franchise.

So much for the one side of the coin. There is another point of view, a compelling one. It is the line held by New Zealand and by England. And it suits their particular circumstance. There is no

ABOVE Ulster's Ruan Pienaar runs into heavy traffic for the Springboks against the Wallabies in 2014's Rugby Championship. South Africa are prepared to pick those who play their club rugby abroad.

FACING PAGE Changes to Australian policy mean that Matt Giteau (left) and Drew Mitchell will be eligible for selection for the Wallabies once again.

absolute ethical line to be drawn here, no black and white, no line in the sand to be drawn and battle stations to be manned at all costs.

This is about pragmatism, about working out what suits and getting on with it. There is a middle way as Wales have found with the so-called Gatland's Law. In fact, head coach Warren Gatland has never laid down precise strictures as to who can and who can't play outside the Principality. Those regulations have been laid down by the joint body of region and union. They are not straightforward. There are exemptions, a couple of wild cards that can be used at any one time. There is also a real sense, though, that Gatland would not allow himself to be denied a star-turn player such as a Leigh Halfpenny or Jamie Roberts no matter what the circumstances might be. Wales have a much smaller playing pool than England, for example, and it would be suicidal for them to ostracise a player for a man-made technicality.

The situation in England is different, as is the case in New Zealand. The Kiwis have fuelled so much of the mythology that suffuses the black shirt, the ritualistic sense of rugby being something elemental and essential for every New Zealander, through veneration of playing for one's country, the small nation at the ends of the earth, that they simply cannot afford for that concept to be diluted. They have had to be innovative as well as flexible to hold that line, allowing the likes of Richie McCaw and Dan Carter to have extended breaks from the game, a sabbatical either to be spent as McCaw prefers in New Zealand itself, or in the case of the more footloose Carter, a stint playing in France for Perpignan. Yet the integrity of their policy has not been compromised. There was no call to arms for Harlequins fly half Nick Evans when their No. 10s all began to keel over during the 2011 Rugby World Cup. The New Zealand union held firm, knowing that one exception would open the floodgates.

And that is exactly where England and the RFU stand, united in their belief that if they countenanced one exemption, within a couple of seasons they would have to be considering multiple such scenarios if they wanted to get their best XV out on the field. There is also a commitment to the English game being made, to the Aviva Premiership in particular, to a desire to protect the status of that competition by having the best English talent on parade each and every week.

Stuart Lancaster also wants to see his contenders go head-to-head with their rivals for an England shirt as often as possible. Is Steffon Armitage a better open-side flanker than Chris Robshaw? We may never get to find out as the two players have not been up against each other in regular club contests for some years.

There is no doubt in my mind that if Lancaster had contrived a way to include Armitage in the 2015 Rugby World Cup there would have been a whole host of transfers opening up in the coming years. The French marketplace is vibrant as well as volatile. It is the most financially fluid in world rugby, akin to football almost, certainly within France. The TV deals are lucrative, while the presence of deep-pocketed moguls willing, and able, to bankroll teams shows no sign of fading.

Lancaster depends on the co-operation of the English clubs to help nurture and develop players. It is a partnership, a symbiotic arrangement. And that is why they are right to protect their product.

Players have a choice. They are well remunerated in that an England contract is worth in the region of £150,000 for a ten-match shift of duty, while a club contract for leading players would be of the order of £250,000. An international place also opens up the possibilities of commercial endorsements.

All a player asks for on the field of play is that officials are consistent. A player wants to know what he can and can't do. It is no different off the field either. Lancaster has stated his case. And he is right to do so, right to hold the line. The policy is the right one.

RIGHT All Black stand-off Dan Carter was granted a sabbatical by New Zealand in 2008, alllowing him to join Perpignan in France's Top 14. In the event, an Achilles injury suffered in the game against Stade Français in Paris at the end of January 2009 (at which this picture was taken) cut his season short.

FACING PAGE New Zealand kept to the rules even when they had a fly half crisis during the 2011 World Cup, meaning no call-up for Harlequins' former All Black Nick Evans.

GREENE KING IPA
THE PERFECT MATCH PINT

OUR HERITAGE, OUR PASSION. YOUR IPA.

GREENE KING
BURY ST EDMUNDS

1799

IPA
INDIA PALE ALE
alc 3.6% vol
WESTGATE BREWERY · 1799

INTERNATIONAL SCENE

Jerry Collins
A Very, Very Good Man

by RAECHELLE INMAN

'But that didn't deter the recent All Black legend, who turned up the following Saturday happily packing down at the back of the scrum for the 2nd XV in a Devon Merit Table match'

Watch any highlights package of Jerry Collins' career and you can feel the hits: huge; intimidating; hard. He put his body on the line. Collins was one of the most feared players of the modern era. In 2003 he left Welsh captain Colin Charvis unconscious after a tackle. It's no wonder he earned nicknames like 'Terminator', 'Hitman' and 'Granite'.

Samoan-born Collins represented New Zealand 48 times, debuting as a 20-year-old in 2001 saying it was 'the biggest thing that could happen to me'.

'Can you be humble and proud at the same time? I think so. That is how it feels,' he said.

He also played eight seasons with the Wellington Hurricanes, amassing an impressive 85 provincial caps.

Tragically Collins and his partner were killed in a car accident in France on 5 June 2015.

His shock passing proved to be an inspiration for the 2015 Wellington Hurricanes in their Super Rugby quest, propelling them to a coveted place in the final against the Otago Highlanders. Although the 'Canes went down 21-14 in that game, the 'Jerry Collins factor' certainly played its part in helping them get there. Before kick-off in their first home game after Collins' death (the Super Rugby semi-final against the Brumbies), a giant No. 6 jersey was unfurled on the pitch. The players also had the initials 'JC' embroidered onto their jumper sleeves. And towards the end of their emphatic 29-9 win, chants of 'Jerry, Jerry' echoed around the stadium.

Captain Conrad Smith said emotions had been raw after the accident: a number of the current players had been team-mates of Collins.

'It's hard to quantify but it is definitely playing its part,' he said.

It appeared that his good mate Ma'a Nonu was channelling Collins in the final, producing an outstanding and powerful game, but unfortunately it wasn't the fairy-tale ending for the Wellington side, who were chasing their maiden title.

When Collins was killed he was only 34 years of age and tributes quickly poured in from all over the rugby world. Charvis said: 'What we are going to remember of Jerry is not only the uncompromising 80 minutes on the pitch but what a heck of a good bloke he was off it.'

Former New Zealand captain Sean Fitzpatrick added: 'We say in the All Blacks that good men make great All Blacks. He was a very, very good man.

'Tough as old boots on the field, but off the field he'd be the nicest guy you'd meet. It's very, very sad news. He'll be remembered fondly.'

From beneath the brutal and tough exterior, an image emerges of a warm, humble and kind soul.

'He'll be remembered as a tough man, but he was way more than that,' said All Blacks coach Steve Hansen.

'He loved the game itself and the camaraderie. He didn't expect anything out of it. Everything he got was a bonus.'

Collins never forgot where he was from or let success go to his head. When he signed his first professional rugby contract, Collins bought his parents a house in the upmarket Porirua suburb of Whitby, while he moved into the working-class state house they left behind in Cannons Creek.

He had grown up in Porirua, a regional city near Wellington, having moved from Samoa to New Zealand as a small boy. He maintained an ongoing interest in and connection to his community.

At 18 years of age, Jerry became the world's youngest captain of a senior club rugby team, for his beloved Norths Rugby Club. He was well known for sneaking out of All Black training camps to play for his club, even as international matches loomed.

An apt story that sheds light on Collins' nature is the one of the lady who regularly sat by the players' tunnel at Hurricanes home games. Collins would wave to her and smile. The lady was Lynley McEwen, his former maths teacher from Tawa College. It was McEwen whom Collins credited with starting him on the journey to become an All Black, after she told his parents that although he was getting good marks at school, he was mucking up in class and suggested he move to St Patrick's College in Wellington. Soon after the switch in schools Collins found himself in the New Zealand Secondary Schools team and being named Player of the Tournament at the Under 19 World Championship in 1999. At St Pat's he earned the nickname 'Chicken Legs', as his ankles were

FACING PAGE Jerry Collins finds something to smile about during the captain's run on the eve of the Tri-Nations/Bledisloe Cup fixture between New Zealand and Australia in Christchurch in July 2006.

always skinny, overshadowed by those hulking arms. At his peak his biceps measured a massive 54 centimetres.

Collins' connection to grass-roots rugby and his genuine love for the game is epitomised in the well-known story of his holiday in Devon in 2007, after the All Blacks had just bowed out of the World Cup in the quarter-finals. It was there he bumped into Kevin Squire, director of rugby at Devon club Barnstaple, who were then playing in the South West 2 West division. Collins asked to play for the club but was told he couldn't play for the first-grade side as he wasn't registered. But that didn't deter the recent All Black legend, who turned up the following Saturday happily packing down at the back of the scrum for the 2nd XV in a Devon Merit Table match against Newton Abbot. At Twickenham a

ABOVE Terminator at work. France lock Jérôme Thion is clattered by Jerry Collins in Paris in November 2004. Collins scored in a game the All Blacks won 45-6.

RIGHT Jerry Collins charges Daniel Vickerman as the All Blacks beat the Wallabies 30-13 in their August 2005 Tri-Nations/Bledisloe Cup clash at Sydney.

month later, Collins represented the Barbarians against South Africa wearing Barnstaple's red socks. 'He wore the socks with pride and put the club on the map,' Squire said.

Collins captained the All Blacks three times – against Argentina in 2006 and then against Portugal and Romania in 2007. 'He was a very intelligent man, but he chose not to always portray that,' said Hansen. 'I always remember the night he captained the All Blacks against Argentina. At the after match he spoke in fluent Spanish,' he continued.

Collins was full of surprises and was a consistent favourite of fans, who loved his ever present magnetic smile, his straight talking, his cheeky sense of humour and his authenticity. For four years, the loose forward ran beside Wellington City Council rubbish trucks for fitness. He didn't want to be paid for his work. He saw it as an education in 'how people treat people'. He threw rubbish for the same people every week, but it wasn't until he became a famous rugby player that anyone really spoke to him.

After leaving the Hurricanes, Collins played for French side Toulon during the 2008-09 season, then in May 2009 agreed a two-year deal to join Welsh team Ospreys, earning the prestigious Players' Player of the Year award in the 2009-10 season. At the beginning of the 2011 season he joined the Yamaha club in Japan.

In a bizarre incident in 2013 Collins was arrested in a Japanese department store after he was spotted carrying a 17cm-long knife. Collins claimed it was for self-defence after he had been threatened by members of a Brazilian gang who objected to his relationship with a woman. Collins tested negative for all illegal substances and was released after agreeing to pay a fine for breaching local regulations on carrying knives. He said that he was 'relieved' to have been arrested, as he had feared for his life.

By many accounts Collins' life wasn't all smooth sailing. After playing for the Classic All Blacks against Fiji in 2013, he took 2014 off rugby, choosing to get away from the limelight in a small town

in prairie Canada, working in the security industry. There he was able to find peace, a partner in Alana Madill and a new life as a family man with baby daughter Ayla.

In January 2015, rugby called again as Collins signed a deal with French second-division club Narbonne, having not played rugby since his stint with Japanese club Yamaha two years earlier. Narbonne president Anthony Hill said Collins single-handedly turned around the club's season to avoid relegation.

'He saved the season really, and I say that without exaggeration,' Hill said.

'He scored a try to get us a bonus point win at one point and scored two tries in a big derby with Perpignan. He was instrumental in changing the club's future.'

Around 1500 people in the southern French city of Narbonne took part in a silent march to honour the lives of Collins and Madill. If he was the kind of foreign player who just turned up for the pay cheque he wouldn't have been given such an emotional farewell by the French.

Sébastien Petit from the club said: 'I feel a lot of sadness and, frankly, I find it hard to believe. I do not have the words but I'm full of images that go through my head. Jerry was next to me in the dressing room. He was a wonderful and endearing type. We can say thank you to him for his contribution.'

At Collins' funeral in his home town of Porirua, his cousin Tana Umaga described him as a unique person with a deep love of rugby who had been revelling in his latest role as a father and family man.

'I rest easy in the knowledge he found love,' Umaga said.

Another former All Black, Chris Masoe, shared with mourners at the funeral service the ultimate sacrifice Collins made in his final moments: he was in the back of the car when the fatal crash happened and he sheltered his daughter with his arms and body. She miraculously survived the impact. 'You made it possible for her to have a chance. That is the man you are,' he said.

Jonah Lomu agreed: 'What they say about how they found him, he was protecting his baby. That's just typical Jerry. When you talk about putting your body on the line, he did that.'

Along with the New Zealand rugby community, we bid farewell to a tough and talented player with a larger than life personality who made a huge impact on our great game.

FACING PAGE, TOP Jerry Collins with Rodney So'oialo (left) and Filipo Levi after New Zealand won the SANZAR/UAR Under 21 Championship in 2000.

FACING PAGE, BOTTOM Jerry Collins and Paul Miller play touch rugby during a grass-roots training session at Blackrock College RFC in Dublin on the All Blacks' 2001 tour.

BELOW A giant No. 6 shirt is unfurled in honour of Jerry Collins before the 2015 Super Rugby semi-final between the Hurricanes and the Brumbies at Wellington's Westpac Stadium.

Back to Black
the World Rugby U20 Championship
by ALAN LORIMER

'Their adventurous style, their precision passing and the sheer personality of what was a stellar cast of players made the Baby Blacks the crowd favourites'

They're back. After a four-year wait New Zealand returned to the top of the global age-grade ladder by winning the World Rugby U20 Championship 2015 in the Lombardy region of Italy to deny beaten finalists England a hat-trick of titles.

The Baby Blacks secured their overall win despite being run dangerously close by Argentina in the pool stage and then being challenged all the way by England in the final. But over the piece, they fully merited the top honour after producing performances full of power, pace and not a little panache that other sides struggled to emulate.

New Zealand's more free-flowing rugby conferred on them a charisma that elevated them above teams reliant on structured and tight forward play. Their adventurous style, their precision passing and the sheer personality of what was a stellar cast of players made the Baby Blacks the crowd favourites. New Zealand believed in the running game, they believed in positive rather than negative rugby and in the end that belief was vindicated.

The Baby Blacks showed their championship-winning potential in round one of the competition with a 68-10 Pool C win over Scotland, in which New Zealand's nine tries were scored by nine

different players. Argentina were next up for the Baby Blacks, but what should have been a relatively straightforward New Zealand win turned out otherwise. Los Pumitas staged a late surge to draw level at 29-29 with only minutes left to play, but a penalty goal by New Zealand fly half Otere Black on the stroke of full-time settled the game.

New Zealand then went on to defeat Ireland 25-3 but failed to score four tries, leaving them one point short of the 15 they needed to claim the top ranking at the end of the pool stage. That prime spot went to South Africa, whose powerful forward pack had blitzed its way through Pool B with wins over Italy (33-5) and Samoa (40-8) and then a sizeable 46-13 victory against Australia.

In Pool A, France and England were the teams to watch. England opened with a 59-7 win over Japan before defeating Wales 30-16. France were able to match England's results and so it then became a matter of which of these two countries would reach the semi-finals.

In the event both got through. France produced an all-round performance to subdue England, their 30-18 victory securing Les Tricolores their semi-final place. England, however, had accumulated ten points from their pool matches, the same total as Australia; but a superior points difference meant the defending champions claimed the fourth semi-final spot.

The conditions in Calvisano were hot and humid for the first of the semi-finals, between

LEFT The Baby Blacks celebrate regaining the junior world crown after defeating England in Cremona.

South Africa and England, in what was expected to be a clash of two big forward packs. And that was how it unfolded. *Strictly Come Dancing* it was not.

With a mountainous set of forwards, South Africa had reckoned that they could bully England by playing a tight game. But it was a miscalculation by the Baby Boks, and in fact it was England who bossed the tight play, scoring two tries from the set-piece, and one from a clever grubber kick by centre Nick Tompkins for a 28-20 win.

France, having played well against England in the pool stage, had reason to be confident about facing New Zealand. But if you had to pick one game to show why the Baby Blacks deserved to be champions, then this was it. The young French side were simply blown away by a hurricane of try-scoring rugby that resulted in an unexpectedly high 45-7 defeat for the cream of French youth. New Zealand wing Tevita Li scored a hat-trick, while back-row Akira Ioane touched down twice.

The Italian Federation had chosen a football ground, the Stadio Giovanni Zini in Cremona, to showcase the rugby final. Fans were anticipating a spectacular ending to the championship and they were not disappointed as two teams playing with contrasting styles showed rugby at its most absorbing.

England had been expected to replicate the tactics used to defeat South Africa, but a clever try through midfield by centre Max Clark revealed a different approach. The game's other first-half try was scored by the New Zealand replacement Vincent Tavae-Aso less than a minute after joining the fray. Two penalty goals by Otere Black to one by Rory Jennings left New Zealand ahead 11-10 at half-time. The gap was extended with a converted try by Akira Ioane, but minutes later the No. 8 was sin-binned for an illegal tackle on Jennings. The England fly half kicked the resultant penalty and then added another to bring the score to 18-16.

Then England suffered a piece of misfortune after the referee (corrrectly) chalked off a 'try' by replacement Piers O'Conor, who had chased a kick ahead by winger Howard Packman. Following consultation with the TMO, referee Will Houston ruled that O'Conor had been in front of the kicker. A third penalty goal by Black stretched the New Zealand lead to 21-16, but late in the game England had a chance to draw level when they drove a line out. The Baby Blacks dug deep to repel England's powerful forward effort and minutes later were celebrating a hard-won victory.

It had been a classic final, and one that went to the wire. On the day, though, New Zealand's team fired on 15 cylinders both in attack and defence, and crucially their Super 15 players were influential. For their part England, the less flashy of the two sides, went in as underdogs but came very close to upsetting the pundits' predictions.

Earlier at Cremona the 2012 champions, South Africa, redeemed themselves with a comfortable 31-18 win over France to claim the third finishing place, while in the fifth-place play-off a strong second half allowed Australia to edge out Wales with a 28-23 victory.

One level down Ireland were 17-9 winners over Scotland thanks to two tries by winger Stephen Fitzgerald, but it was a tired performance from both sides and in no small way due to the Celtic nations' greater difficulty in adapting to the very hot and humid conditions that marred the early rounds.

At the lower end of the championship Argentina, who earlier in the year had won a warm-up Test against South Africa, finished a disappointing ninth, a position that represented underperformance by Los Pumitas. Argentina were undone by two bad results in the pool stage, a 18-16 defeat to Ireland, after the Irish had kicked an 80th-minute penalty goal from the touch line, and then by a shock 29-6 defeat to Scotland. That meant Argentina, for a second successive year, were amongst the bottom four countries. In the event the young Pumas romped past Italy and then Japan in the final two rounds.

For the host country, Italy, relegation became the issue in the last round. The Azzurri, however, achieved one of the great escapes by winning 20-19 against Samoa. That resulted in the Pacific Islanders dropping out of the championship for next year and joining fellow islanders Fiji and Tonga in the trophy competition.

Exciting though it is to watch the actual matches, identifying stars of the future is another occupation for spectators. In that context a number of players from the 2015 New Zealand team looked destined to become All Blacks, among them lock Joshua Goodhue and back-row players Blake Gibson, Mitchell Dunshea and Akira Ioane from the forwards, and scrum half Te Toiroa Tahuriorangi, fly half Otere Black and centre TJ Faiane in the back line.

From the England side, prop Ellis Genge, fly half Rory Jennings and centres Max Clark and Nick Tompkins all impressed, while from third-placed South Africa more will heard about locks Jason Jenkins and RG Snyman and fly half Brandon Thomson.

Elsewhere full back Jonah Placid (Australia), centre Owen Watkin, wing Joshua Adams and flanker Ollie Griffiths (all Wales), fly half Joey Carbery and centres Sam Arnold and Garry Ringrose (all Ireland), and centre Bautista Ezcurra (Argentina) caught the eye.

In terms of progress in the rankings, Japan who jumped from twelfth to tenth and Scotland who finished in a highest ever position of eighth achieved most. Scotland's advancement was especially creditable considering that 15 of the Scottish squad are eligible for next year's tournament and moreover that they lost their top second-row, Lewis Carmichael, cited for an alleged 'hand-near-the-eye' incident in a maul and given an overly harsh nine-week suspension. Additionally Scotland were hit by a two-match suspension imposed on their centre Archie Russell for a supposedly dangerous tackle against New Zealand.

BELOW The final. New Zealand were only 18-16 ahead when this acrobatic finish by England replacement Piers O'Conor was disallowed for O'Conor having been offside earlier in the move.

The World Rugby U20 Championship will return to the United Kingdom after an eight-year gap for the 2016 tournament, hosted by Manchester at Sale Sharks' AJ Bell Stadium and the Manchester City Academy Stadium. Cooler climes certainly, but the competition surely will be just as hot.

Toulouse Jamboree
the Rugby Europe U18 Championship
by CHRIS THAU

'However, the limelight of the opening day was stolen by Georgia and Italy. The former knocked Ireland out of the medal race in a penalty shoot-out following their 8-8 draw'

ABOVE The France Under 18 side celebrate victory in the Elite Division final with a selfie.

There was a sense of occasion among both organisers and participants at the 2015 Rugby Europe U18 Championship, which kicked off in the Midi-Pyrénées region of France on 27 March. The tournament, the world's largest age-group competition, had offered an appropriate stage for the celebrations of 80 years since the formation of Rugby Europe's forerunner, the Fédération Internationale de Rugby Amateur, better known by its acronym of FIRA. The establishment of FIRA was the beginning of organised rugby on the Continent, offering the European nations a playing framework, which enabled them to express their rugby prowess and ambitions.

In the 1960s FIRA became increasingly active and in 1969 it launched, in Madrid, an Under 19 tournament, the first age-group tournament in the world. Over the years the FIRA Under 19 tournament, which became the cornerstone of rugby development in Europe, has changed its name, shape and structure a number of times. In 2004 it split into an Under 19 World Championship, the forefather of today's World Rugby U20 Championship, and the current European Under 18 tournament, initially organised by FIRA-AER, and from this year onwards by its successor Rugby Europe.

The pioneering FIRA Under 19 tournament in Spain, which had only six participants, has now grown into the biggest rugby tournament in international rugby, gathering 24 unions, represented by over 600 players under the age of 18, playing 36 matches in three divisions (Elite, A and B), over 11 days of competition. Mind you, there are a further two divisions, C and D, which cater for developing unions; tournaments which are held elsewhere – this year in Hungary and Andorra respectively.

Toulouse, the legendary capital of the Midi–Pyrénées region, and its neighbouring towns and villages, one of the most fertile nurseries of French rugby, hosted this year's tournament. Often compared with its senior counterpart, the RWC tournament, the Under 18 event is an international tournament with a difference. Due to the unpredictable nature of age-group selection, which varies from one year to another, upsets are a common occurrence and the champions keep changing. However, consistent elite age-group development is usually rewarded at all levels of the European behemoth, as the twelfth tournament confirmed.

The essence of the event was captured in the opening address of Rugby Europe president Octavian Morariu. 'For most of you, the 600-odd teenage participants, this will remain a highlight of your early rugby career, while for some this could become a step towards a professional rugby career. However, irrespective of your prowess and ambitions, irrespective if you win or lose, this tournament will be for all of you an educational experience. It is about winning with dignity and losing with grace, it is about the spirit of the game that has enabled us to pass the game from generation to generation, mindful of its values and traditions,' he said.

The Elite Division kicked off in spectacular fashion. Trophy holders England made an emphatic statement of intent with a 13-try (85-5) demolition of Portugal in Montauban, while France defeated a gallant Scotland team 22-10 in Graulhet. The final score somewhat flattered Scotland, who battled bravely to stem the tide of French attacks. With their scrummage cracking under the enormous pressure generated by the French, it was through the loose and line out, with skipper Callum Hunter-Hill making a significant contribution, that the Scots managed to stay in the game.

RIGHT Italy Under 18 replacement scrum half Matteo Maria Panunzi stands by to put the ball in against Wales in a match the Italians took by a single point, 14-13.

FACING PAGE France on the attack against Georgia in the Elite Division final, which the home side won 57-0.

However, the limelight of the opening day was stolen by Georgia and Italy. The former knocked Ireland out of the medal race in a penalty shoot-out following their 8-8 draw after 70 minutes of play. It was one of those days when the proverbial luck deserted the Irish, who failed with three of their four kicks at goal, while the beaming Georgians seemed to get everything right. Meanwhile, a competent and hard-working Italy firing on all cylinders managed to upset (14-13) a Welsh team who were unable to control the game despite their perceived superior pedigree and experience.

The format employed in the U18 Championship requires each match to have a winner and a loser to enable the tournament to proceed. The match winner moves into the next round of knockout matches, while the loser is demoted to a play-down structure against the other losers. In round two (semi-final), Georgia pulled another rabbit out of the hat, as they managed to draw 6-6 with the Italians and sneak through to the tournament final following another penalty shoot-out. Luck of the Georgians! A scoreless draw, the third of the competition, was the outcome of the Portugal v Scotland play-down semi-final, with the Portuguese winning the penalty shoot-out 3-2.

Wales recaptured some of the confidence dented by the Italians in the earlier round and managed to defeat Ireland 14-9 in their round two match to secure themselves a place in the play-off for fifth position. In that game the Welsh put Portugal to the sword 38-8 in a performance full of skill and creativity, while Ireland defeated Scotland 21-12 in their third round match to finish seventh in the overall table. England, who were unlucky to lose 23-19 to France in their semi-final, scoring three tries to France's two, overwhelmed Italy 39-12 in the third round to win the bronze medal. The final itself was a one-way boulevard, with the French, captained by a remarkably mature and talented Alexandre Roumat, son of former French skipper Olivier Roumat, scoring nine tries to Georgia's three yellow cards to run out 57-0 winners.

The first four double-headers featuring the 16 teams of the second (A) and third (B) divisions of the Rugby Europe U18 Championship were held on Saturday 28 March at four rugby clubs in the

Toulouse area – Bruguières, Pamiers, L'Union and Ramonville – with both the visiting teams and Rugby Europe officials praising the immaculate match arrangements. In a one-sided contest, in which keeping track of the mounting score was the main occupational hazard of the match officials, Division A top seeds Russia scored 72 unanswered points against newly promoted Sweden to advance into the next round. Coached by the duo of Raphaël Saint-André and Evgeny Mochnev and orchestrated by talented outside half Gleb Farkov, the Russians were quick to state their intentions, with the first of their 12 tries scored by hooker Artem Kriukov after less than a minute of play. Though the magnitude of the score might flatter the winners, it looks as if this is a particularly gifted Russian generation, with plenty to offer long term. Indeed they went on to beat Germany 23-0 and Belgium 16-0 to finish the tournament undefeated and having not conceded a point (the latter a fairly rare occurrence) to qualify for the Elite Division next season.

The first and most significant upset of the Division A opening day was the narrow 15-14 defeat of third seeds Spain by sixth–ranked Belgium, in a match full of excitement and drama at the Stade de Loudes in L'Union. It was a contest of contrasting styles and methods, with the Spanish playing a high-risk, speedy game against a Belgium side that had both the pace and the size to frustrate their attacking ploys. Romania flattered to deceive in the opening round when they defeated a surprisingly resilient Netherlands 26-0, only to lose to both Belgium (10-3) and Germany (11-10) in the subsequent rounds to finish fourth. Belgium, one of the pleasant surprises of the Division A tournament, reached the final but were cut down to size by the rampant Russians. Spain finished fifth after a 38-0 demolition of Poland, while Sweden will return to Division B after losing 46-8 to a fired-up Netherlands.

In Division B, Lithuania secured a 22-17 upset win over Luxembourg in round one, followed by a 9-0 defeat of Switzerland in round two. However, their luck ran out in the final against a bruising Ukraine, who won 43-8 in an emphatic manner, having previously defeated Serbia (28-3) and the Czech Republic (19-17). The Czechs finished third by beating Switzerland 25-13.

Simply asset management.

Aberdeen Asset
Management is proud
to support Wooden
Spoon, the children's
charity of rugby.

Of No Fixed Abode
125 Years of the
Barbarians
by CHRIS THAU

'There had been nothing like that before in our lives. It was new and exciting. You wanted to be there, and you behaved yourself, because you wanted badly to be invited again'

As the celebrations of the 125th anniversary of the birth of the Barbarian Football Club enter full swing, spare a thought for the club's sixth president, Micky Steele-Bodger, who this year also celebrates his 90th birthday and 28 years since he took over the club without a fixed abode. The man is a rugby polymath of such enthusiasm and energy as to make people half his age seemed drained and worn out.

ABOVE The Barbarians at Twickenham in 2015. Deon Fourie is brought down by Mathew Tait of England.

Micky Steele-Bodger CBE, born in 1925, became the sixth Barbarians president in 1988, having succeeded Scotland legend Herbert Waddell. He started playing at Rugby School and made a name for himself during his two Varsity Match appearances for Cambridge University immediately after the war, in 1945 and 1946. The first invitation for the 20-year-old to play for the Barbarians was in the Mobbs Memorial Match against East Midlands, in February 1946, when he made a strong impression with his pace and fierce tackling. Six weeks later he joined the Barbarians at their Easter Tour base at the Esplanade Hotel in Penarth, a place that won his perpetual affection. Steele-Bodger proceeded to make the second of his 13 Barbarians appearances (two as captain) on Good Friday 1946 against the local club and finished the South Wales tour against Swansea three days later.

From then on everything in his life happened with a speed commensurate with his breakneck forays in the loose. He was selected by England and played with distinction for two seasons, winning nine caps, while he moved to Edinburgh University to finish his veterinary studies. His attention to detail and organised mind were noted by Emile de Lissa, who asked him to join the club committee during his first South Wales tour. This was the period in which he got acquainted with four of his five predecessors – de Lissa; H.A. 'Jack' Haigh Smith, who died after only a few months in the job; Brigadier Hugh Llewellyn Glyn Hughes, a highly decorated war hero; and former Scotland and Lions great Herbert Waddell. When Glyn Hughes became club president, Steele-Bodger, by that time sidelined by a nasty knee injury, took over as secretary. He took to his new admin duties like a duck to water.

'For us the Barbarians Easter tour was an absolute blessing. There were no international tours at the time, and the Lions tours were quite infrequent, so the Barbarians were the next best thing. Also, from 1933 France was no longer in the picture, so for the keen young men selected, the Barbarians was the thing. They were also the kind of people with whom you could spend the whole night discussing rugby tactics and I remember Jika Travers using the table cloth at the Esplanade

Hotel to draw diagrams. There had been nothing like that before in our lives. It was new and exciting. You wanted to be there, and you behaved yourself, because you wanted badly to be invited again. On the other hand, though the standard was very high, there was not so much pressure as there was when playing for England,' recalled Steele-Bodger.

'In 1948 I got selected for the first Barbarians match against an international side at the end of the Australian tour. They had a very good tour and the press had gone overboard, calling the match the "match of the century". We were not impressed at all. It was desperately pompous. We did not want all that pressure of playing in the "match of the century", so we talked to the Australians and asked them to come for a drink to our hotel. We were staying at the Angel in Cardiff and the

ABOVE The Barbarians v Australia, 1948. Back row (l to r): F. Trott, K. Mullen, I. Henderson, M.F. Turner, W.I.D. Elliott, S.V. Perry, W.E. Tamplin, H. Walker, C.B. Holmes; Seated: J. Mycock, H. Tanner (c), H.A. Haigh Smith (V-P), E. de Lissa (Pres), Brig H.L. Glyn Hughes (Sec), T.A. Kemp, B.L. Williams; Front: W.B. Clever, M.R. Steele-Bodger.

LEFT England v France, Twickenham, 1947. Micky Steele-Bodger in hot pursuit of Elie Pebeyre.

Wallabies stayed at the Esplanade in Penarth. The Australians came over and we had a hell of a party. They challenged us to do a bit of live scrummaging, and a few chairs and a palm pot got damaged, but we had great time. It was quite a do, and in fact the following night after the match was just as good,' Steele-Bodger added.

His thirteenth and last Barbarians match was against Leicester on 27 December 1949. His playing career ended when he ruptured his cruciate ligaments during training before a game against Moseley a few weeks later. With his playing career in tatters, Steele-Bodger threw himself wholeheartedly into the game's administration, while working hard to build his veterinary practice. He carried on as Barbarians secretary, and became an England selector in 1953 – at the age of 28, the youngest ever – a position he retained for 15 years. He became president of the RFU in 1973, after which he became a member of the IRFB Council, which he chaired in 1985.

To better understand the Barbarian tribe and what makes them tick, one has to recall the Right Reverend Walter Julius Carey of 1896 Lions fame and one of the 1890 Barbarians originals, who inadvertently became the chief ideologist of the club when he coined his famous phrase 'Rugby Football is a game for gentlemen of all classes, but never for a bad sportsman of any class'. This statement has become a mandatory code of standards for the club's members, irrespective of their upbringing, race, colour or creed; very much an early statement about the inclusiveness of rugby football.

In the words of former *Times* correspondent O.L. Owen, 'the order of the Barbarians, which costs nothing, may now be conferred upon any rugby-playing citizen of the Empire, if he is not lacking in manners and sportsmanship'. This mantra has acquired additional significance during the last two decades, when winning-at-all costs attitudes and the gamesmanship associated with them have eroded some of the traditional values attached to the game.

However, while Carey's ethical slogan has had an impact on the deeds and manners of the Barbarian recruits, making a great contribution to the evolution of the 'spirit of the game' concept, there has been no clear explanation of their decision to adopt a playing style, which was very much at odds with the outlook of the era. It is difficult to ascertain why Andrew Stoddart and his team-mates decided to play for each other, rather than let their 'individual brilliance' do the talking, in the Barbarians' first game, against Hartlepool Rovers on 27 December 1890, in a style that became the club's hallmark. Was this a deliberate decision taken in April at the Southern Nomads oyster supper hosted by the Barbarians' founder Percy Carpmael at Leuchters Restaurant in Bradford, or was it an afterthought, perhaps the outcome of one of the earliest 'rugby debating societies' the club had become famous for?

With the Hartlepool press seemingly oblivious to the emergence of the new Barbarians club, the only information about the match that created history comes from the local club's records. 'It was a splendid exposition and one of the best matches I have seen, and as an object lesson it ought to have been witnessed by all other players … Individual brilliancy may have its merits, but the game is intended for a team,' wrote the anonymous chronicler. Mostly by word of mouth and also by personal example, the new Barbarians approach caught the imagination of the rugby public, keen to escape the clutches of the interminable forward battles of the era.

The first match in Wales was against Cardiff the following year, while the Newport fixture commenced in 1893. By 1900 the Barbarians had become regular visitors to both Arms Park and Rodney Parade, and as Easter seemed an appropriate time to expand the two-match venture, in 1901 they added both Swansea and Penarth to what for threequarters of a century became known as the Easter Tour of South Wales. The tour opener took place against Penarth on Good Friday, followed by the match against Cardiff on Easter Saturday, golf on Easter Sunday and Swansea on Easter Monday, with Newport, or occasionally Devonport Albion, on Tuesday at the end of the tour.

Three years into Steele-Bodger's presidency, the Barbarians celebrated the club's centenary. His words during the centenary season are equally valid now, on its 125th anniversary.

'We are very fortunate to have reached our Centenary in the same state of good health and good cheer as that with which we set out under Percy Carpmael, 100 years ago, as a rugby touring club. We are as famous now as we have ever been and are still doing what we believe is a good job for rugby football in that we allow great players to play for us and to entertain without the pressures of international matches. They like to take part. They do us proud. We enjoy their company and we certainly enjoy their rugby as played on the field.

'However, as a club we do not intend to stand still and simply reflect on a glorious first century. We are proud of what we have achieved so far, we are proud of our name, but we know that we have a mission and a responsibility to the game of rugby football. In achieving our goals whilst preserving the unique character of our club we know we have another 100 years ahead of us that will be just as exciting a challenge.'

For business.
For family.
For life.

Wealth is made of much more than money –
it is realising hopes and dreams, passions
and partnerships. At Arbuthnot Latham we
strive to see beyond the obvious to help
you achieve what really matters.

t: 020 7012 2500   arbuthnotlatham.co.uk

HOME FRONT

A Coventry Tale
Wasps at the Ricoh Arena
by CHRIS JONES

'Next season promises to be a special one for upwardly mobile Wasps, although they have landed in the toughest European Rugby Champions Cup pool'

Dai Young, the Wasps director of rugby, was reduced to putting his hand in his own pocket to pay for medical tape for matches during the club's darkest days while based at Adams Park in High Wycombe. The terms of a ground share with Wycombe Wanderers left the former European champions unable to generate the money to regain lost ground, and the vultures were circling.

That is why the smile Young wore midway through last season was so wide as he looked out onto the Ricoh Arena pitch and tried to take in the most dramatic change in fortunes any rugby club had ever experienced, following their move to Coventry.

Thanks to the drive and determination of owner Derek Richardson, who saved the club from bankruptcy, and the expertise of Nick Eastwood, who has become deputy chairman after masterminding the move to the Midlands as Wasps CEO, Young and his squad of players are now part of a rugby operation that currently has the second-largest turnover of any club outfit in Europe. Richardson is confident they will usurp Toulouse and claim top spot in the near future thanks to business opportunities that have come with the purchase of the Ricoh Arena.

To ensure links are maintained with the club's past success, former player Mark Rigby has taken on the role of club president, while Chris Wright, who owned Wasps during the era when they won 11 trophies in 11 years, remains honorary life president.

Coventry City FC continue to play at the Ricoh Arena – which will have a new high-tech pitch for next season – to the delight of locals who initially had concerns that the relocation

of one of London's most revered rugby clubs to the Midlands would signal real problems for the Sky Blues football operation and Coventry RFC – one of the great names of the amateur game, now overshadowed by their professional neighbours.

Wasps have worked hard to win as many hearts and minds as possible, and while many predicted that Wasps fans (crowds only ever averaged 6000 for home games at Adams Park) would not make the journey up the M40, there is evidence to prove this has not been the case. More importantly, attendances of more than 20,000 became the norm during the second half of a tumultuous season which saw Wasps qualify for the European Champions Cup – vital for their status in the sport.

On top of Young's success with his team – featuring captain and England World Cup flanker James Haskell and powerhouse No. 8 Nathan Hughes – the off-the-field triumphs have been even more head-turning. A new 15-year extension to the existing partnership between Compass Group UK & Ireland and Arena Coventry Ltd (ACL), the club's

BELOW Packed stands in evidence at the Ricoh Arena, Coventry, ahead of Wasps Premiership clash with Leicester in May 2015.

subsidiary company, which runs the Ricoh Arena, is expected to generate £195 million in total turnover at their new home which can boast a 32,000-seater sports stadium; a leading concert venue of 42,500 capacity that has previously hosted Coldplay, Oasis, Take That and Bruce Springsteen; a 6000-square-metre indoor facility that can host 12,000 people for exhibitions, conferences and concerts; a 121-bedroom hotel; and a casino, numerous hospitality suites and two restaurants.

Wasps raised £35 million from an oversubscribed rights issue which has allowed them to clear the debts created by years of failure at Adams Park and also by the purchase of the Ricoh Arena. Multimillion-pound deals have continued to be made and that has enabled Young to start shopping for new players at the top end of the market rather than in the bargain section. Australian flanker George Smith is just the latest new recruit to the ranks and he will, within 18 months, be able to train at the new state-of-the-art facility that the club is planning to build in Coventry to replace their current Acton base in London.

The return from a serious neck injury of Joe Launchbury, the England lock who has signed a new contract to stay at Wasps, also boosted a club that has made such an impact in the Midlands that Leicester felt the need to pay for a large billboard advert extolling their own heritage in the area just to ensure the new neighbours didn't get above themselves!

However, having pulled off a remarkable transformation, Wasps owner Richardson has every right to be bullish and said: 'Combining our turnover with the Ricoh turnover means we are already the largest rugby turnover

FACING PAGE, TOP A relaxed-looking Dai Young at the Ricoh Arena after a training session a few days before Wasps' debut match at the ground in December 2014.

FACING PAGE, BOTTOM 21 December 2014. Nathan Hughes leaves Shane Geraghty in his wake as Wasps beat London Irish 48-16 in their first match at their new ground in front of a Premiership record home crowd of 28,254.

RIGHT Wasps lock Joe Launchbury in action against Northampton in September 2014 before being sidelined from late October until May with a neck injury. The England international has agreed to stay at Wasps.

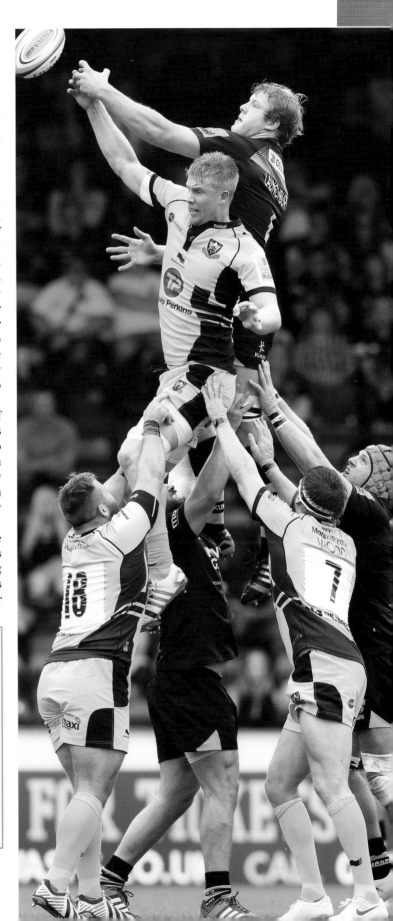

business in the country and second in Europe. We believe with our plan we will be overtaking the top turnover rugby business in Europe within the next two to three years.

'The long term aim is to have the most successful venue and rugby business in Europe. We have the most extensive multi-purpose facility anywhere in Europe and we believe that will be a very important thing for us to maximise. If you look at the Premiership at the moment the only clubs that make money are the clubs that own their own venue. None of the clubs that own their own venue have the extensive facilities we have. I'm very positive for the future.

'Television revenue is going up substantially over the next couple of years, it's on a serious upward curve – as is rugby. Professional rugby is only 20 years old and we believe there will be a great deal more traction in the next 20 than the first 20.'

Next season promises to be a special one for upwardly mobile Wasps, although they have landed in the toughest European Rugby Champions Cup pool, facing Bath Rugby, Toulon and Leinster Rugby.

'We're pretty lucky really, because we could've got a tough group,' joked Young. 'Instead, we only drew the defending European Champions for the past three years, Toulon, three time European Champions Leinster and last season's Aviva Premiership finalists, Bath!

BELOW Wallaby legend George Smith, here representing the Barbarians against England at Twickenham in May, joins Wasps for the 2015-16 season.

'To be serious though, I imagine in many people's eyes we're up against it, but with the journey we're on, the only way to get better is to challenge ourselves against the best teams and you can't get much better can you? We already know these will be brilliant European occasions for our fans to enjoy as well, which is really important.'

England's Rock Star
100 Not Out for Rochelle Clark

by SARA ORCHARD

'I would play for England until I was 60 if I was allowed. I don't think that's going to happen but I will do everything in my power to be at the top of my game come 2017'

Jason Leonard holds the record as England's most capped player, with 114 appearances. However, his record is under threat. In the summer of 2015, at the Rugby Super Series in Canada, England Women's Rochelle Clark stepped out against the USA to win her 101st cap. It made her the most capped English woman of all time, having surpassed hooker Amy Garnett's 100-cap haul. By the end of the tour Clark had 103 caps.

The 34-year-old, known as 'Rocky' or 'Rock Star' to her team-mates, makes no disguise of her desire to hold the overall England record: 'Jason Leonard was a childhood hero of mine and to actually be talked about in any shape or form near him is unbelievable. I often get referred to as the Jason Leonard of women's rugby and I'd just love to be England's most capped player.'

Whilst Clark works towards the 114-cap milestone, the world champion has more than proved her worth on and off the rugby field. In the past 12 months she helped England lift their first Women's Rugby World Cup in 20 years. She and the team then went on to win the BBC Sports Personality Team of the Year award. In 2015 the prop collected her 100th cap in England's final Six Nations match against France at Twickenham, and as the season drew to a close she was named *The Sunday Times* England Women's Player of the Year at the Rugby Players' Association awards. The accolades were finally topped off with a trip to Windsor Castle to collect her MBE from Princess Anne.

'It's been the best year of my life – nothing will come close to this,' said Clark. 'Winning the World Cup was just the start. Adding everything else onto this – I keep saying it's the

icing on the cake but there has been a lot of icing. My mum was doing cartwheels about me getting an MBE; she was so excited and spent a ridiculous amount of money on a frock for herself. It's a fairy tale.'

The awards and accolades come from an England career spanning back to 2003. The then England coach Geoff Richards called Clark to say she'd missed out on an England A tour to South Africa as he wanted her to step up to the senior side on the Churchill Cup tour.

The Amersham-born prop knows that her first cap against Canada shaped her future: 'It was a really tough game. It was 35 degrees, really, really hot and so fast. The only time I touched the ball was when it got fumbled in a line out and it sort of bounced up into my hands so I just ran as quick as I could carrying it forward. The speed of it all was something I'd never experienced, I thought I was going to have a heart attack.

'I can remember Geoff saying afterwards: "Rocky well done, but you've got a lot of work to do to make this *your* spot'. I was like yes I'll do anything I have to do, because that was the life I wanted to lead. I was 17½ stone, I knew I would never play again unless I sorted my fitness out and got my weight down. I thank Geoff for giving me that opportunity and dangling the carrot to help make me the person I am today.'

One of of Clark's everlasting memories from that first tour was spending time with the senior players: 'I can remember this really insane moment being sat on this minibus with all these people around me who where my role models – they were like celebrities to me. That's just such an amazing moment; I'd joined the club. Although I hadn't earned the right to stay in it, it still was a brilliant time.'

After 12 years with England's Red Roses, Clark has seen many players come and go; however, they all have to bear the same initiation after their debuts. She remembers hers, cringing throughout: 'When you get your first cap you have to wear it all night. You also have to sing on the bus on the way back, which is mortifying and humiliating as I have an awful voice. I sang "When Skies are Grey". It was just a horrendous experience but one I'm glad everyone has to do as well.'

Testament to Clark's commitment to rugby is her appearance in three World Cup finals. The third time lucky cliché is apt, but the experiences of previous defeats shaped her determination and refusal to quit.

Her first final was in Canada in 2006 against England's old foe New Zealand. Clark recalls the 25-17 loss as a shock: 'We'd trained so hard and the team had bonded really well – we'd won the Six Nations. Going into the final I truly thought we were going to win and I'd have put my house on it. At the final whistle I knew I'd played well, but I'd had my heart ripped out into a thousand pieces.'

In 2010 the Women's Rugby World Cup was hosted by England, with the final at a sold-out Twickenham Stoop. England would clash with New Zealand once more, but Clark admits she was, for a second time, convinced of victory: 'Again, I would have put my house on it and I thought we were a much better team than 2006. Losing 13-10 by a penalty kick I got my heart ripped out again – a very bizarre feeling because obviously I'd been through it before. It's a bit like your first break-up, you never think you're going to get over it, so the second time round I was seeing the likes of Sophie Hemming lose their first World Cup final and it wasn't as bad as the first time for me – but it was still awful. That was the moment I vowed that I'd be about for the next one to make it right again.'

Success finally came for the loose-head at France 2014. However, it was the first time she wasn't convinced of the result: 'It was the least confident I'd been about a World Cup. We'd had a mixed Six Nations and an odd season with the Sevens girls in and out of the squad. What I did know was that we could win it. Rather than the other two times when I'd said we were guaranteed to win it. I actually think that put us in a better place.'

ABOVE For services to rugby. Rochelle Clark MBE after her investiture by The Princess Royal at Windsor Castle in July 2015.

In the final England met Canada at the Stade Jean Bouin in central Paris to finally stand on top of the world. Clark was well supported by friends and family in Paris. As she was an RFU Level 3 coach for Chesham Stags men's side and Bucks University, many players and fans also made the trip across the Channel. Some even made masks of her face to wear. For those that didn't make the journey, there was a party held in honour of Clark and her England team-mate and fellow coach Kat Merchant at Chesham Stags rugby club: 'The whole of that clubhouse was rammed full, over 100 people all watching the final and supporting us. They even had the local media down as well.'

The 21-9 victory finally gave Clark her long-awaited 'world champion' moniker: 'We just did enough. With Emily Scarratt wearing her kicking boots, and her try, she secured the deal for us. It's hard to explain but imagine a bottle of champagne when you take the cork out and it was just an explosion of emotion and being so happy.

'For the two months afterwards every day I'd wake up and say to myself – you're a world champion, oh my God. It's something that will live with me forever and even sat here talking about it, I'm smiling.'

Clark remains committed to England despite watching many of her fellow World Cup winners retire after their success. She jokes about being called 'Grandpa' during training sessions but has a determination to pass on her knowledge to others: 'I like to help and bring young players on. It does probably help that I'm a bit older with quite a few caps.'

The Worcester prop had always said she'd never retire until she was a world champion. However, now there is a new target: 'My long-term goal is to become a double world champion – that would be amazing. I would play for England until I was 60 if I was allowed. I don't think that's going to happen but I will do everything in my power to be at the top of my game come 2017 in that World Cup.'

Look out Jason Leonard, your days as England's most capped player could be numbered – Clark is after your record.

Dean's New Worcester
Sixways Prepares for the Big Time

by NEALE HARVEY

'Then, as the clock ticked down and tensions at a sold-out Sixways reached fever pitch, the ball was whipped left and Pennell scooted around the cover to touch down'

When Worcester Warriors were relegated from the Aviva Premiership at the end of the 2013-14 season, their talismanic England full back Chris Pennell faced a stark choice: should he turn his back on his boyhood club, the place he called 'home', to pursue his fledgling international ambitions with a so-called bigger team, or would he be better off in the long term by nailing his colours to the mast and buying into director of rugby Dean Ryan's vision of turning the Warriors into a force?

Pennell was not short of offers, with most of England's top clubs keen to acquire his services, but the 28-year-old followed his instincts and stayed put, signing a new three-year deal. Fast-forward a year and it seemed like a poor decision. Trailing Bristol by 13 points on aggregate with just eight minutes of their Championship play-off

BELOW Chris Pennell slips away from Nicky Robinson's tackle to touch down in the dying moments of the second leg of the Championship final. Now it was up to Ryan Lamb ...

second leg remaining, it looked as though the Warriors, along with the crestfallen Pennell, were destined to spend another year in English rugby's second tier.

But then came the miracle to end all miracles as one of the most dramatic comebacks you are likely to see unfolded. First, a penalty try as Worcester hauled themselves off the canvas to put doubts in Bristolian minds. Then, as the clock ticked down and tensions at a sold-out Sixways reached fever pitch, came deliverance as Warriors put the shove on a short-range scrum, the ball was whipped left and Pennell – who else? – scooted around the cover to touch down near the posts.

Ryan Lamb's conversion sailed through, tying the match 30-30 on the night and giving Worcester a 59-58 victory over the two legs, leaving Pennell to reflect on a priceless one-point margin: 'It was an incredible effort and I couldn't be prouder of this group of men. It was 11 months of hard work and that was the justification for it right there at the end. It justifies all the tough decisions you make in life and we've come so far together. It's a journey and the belief we have is amazing.'

Good fortune or not – and the defeated men of Bristol could be heard grumbling long into the night about the unfairness of it all after having two men yellow-carded late on – Pennell has come to symbolise the 'new Worcester'. The Warriors team of old tended to be populated with ageing stars who were more interested in a pay day, but Ryan, in his second year in charge, has begun the process of ridding the Sixways side of that image and here was the living proof.

Pennell is now central to that, with Ryan explaining: 'I can't speak highly enough of Chris. When I came here I recognised his importance and loyalty to Worcester, but I also felt his frustration that Worcester wasn't going the way he wanted it to. He wasn't going to allow his loyalty to overtake his ambition but he recognised that I and the people around me had track records of doing it at top Premiership clubs and that we wanted him to be right in the middle of what we do.

'He was fed up after six or seven years of it not being right but he made a great statement when he said, "I'd hate you to get this right and me not to be involved in it". That's what we've done with GJ van Velze, Jonathan Thomas and Phil Dowson, too, and at the end of the four or five years we will hopefully work together, I want Chris to sit down and say, "I made the right decision".'

Ryan's job now is to make Worcester a respected top-flight team, and while he has made some astute signings, with Dowson arriving from Northampton and the exciting winger Bryce Heem from the Waikato Chiefs, where he impressed in Super Rugby, growth will largely be organic, with home-grown players like Max Stelling, Andy Symons, Ben Howard and Val Rapava Ruskin given a chance to shine. The days of boom and bust are over; this time Ryan is determined to make it stick.

'We've stopped people saying they are going to Worcester because it's a Premiership club, they're coming here now because of what we're trying to do and are prepared to take the risks that go with it,' said the former England back-row forward. 'That's given us people that really care about the place. It's maybe made us miss out on some talent as well but it's been one of the really important DNA parts that we set out from day one. We've got to do our next two or three bits of recruitment business on the same basis and if we can't do that, we won't be doing any business.

'We've got a little bit of recruitment space because of the World Cup but we've also got to be careful about how we treat the other players already at the club. I've sat down with every one of them and sold them their chance of playing in the Premiership, and I'm not going to take that away because so and so is available because Saracens or Leicester are simply fed up with them. We'll maintain what we set out to do 18 months ago and give our own players like Symons, Stelling, Howard and Rapava Ruskin an opportunity to develop in the Premiership. They're going to find it difficult but let's see if we can support them to develop and get better.'

FACING PAGE Dean Ryan, director of rugby at Sixways, is under no illusions how tough the 2015-16 season will be.

BELOW In action here for Worcester Cavaliers in the Aviva 'A' League, former England Under 20 international Ben Howard understudied the injured Chris Pennell to great effect in 2014-15, scoring seven tries in 23 first-team appearances.

Those ideals are fine, but Ryan is no fool. He knows the Aviva Premiership is an unforgiving arena, adding: 'If anyone is running ahead with their expectations, this year is going to be the toughest Premiership year ever. There's a World Cup which means there's no LV= Cup, which means there's no breathing space and, as a promoted club, that can suffocate you.

'The expectations are to try and grow, be credible and hold ourselves together. We're under no illusions as to what the challenge is and no illusions that it's beyond anything we experienced in the Championship. It's an incredibly physical league and the top end is phenomenal both in intensity and standard. To be able to break Worcester's cycle from being a ninth-to-twelfth-placed team to being in the top six or seven is a huge challenge.'

The good news for Worcester, however, is that promotion will boost their bank account. The club lost a staggering £5.4 million in season 2013-14, but with central income on the rise and the possibility of at least five guaranteed seasons in the top flight as a result of the Premiership's desire to expand to 14 teams and suspend relegation, chief executive Jim O'Toole is expecting a cash windfall.

He explained: 'Short-term, we'll receive an immediate injection of £4.5 million in central funding this season and, on top of that, I estimate gates will rise by 3000-4000 and sponsorship, hospitality, merchandise and bar sales will increase as well. There are discussions going on at Premiership Rugby level about ring-fencing, so it means Ryan Lamb's kick could end up being worth over £25 million.

'People don't want to watch relegated teams in the Championship, they want to see the big teams and with five derby-type matches next season against Leicester, Northampton, Wasps, Bath and Gloucester, that will boost season ticket sales and help us balance those books.'

Worcester are back and this time they intend to stay, while the talented Pennell can doubtless look forward to renewing acquaintance with the white shirt of England.

RIGHT A fairy tale for Worcester; a nightmare for Bristol. Ryan Lamb wheels away after slotting the conversion of Chris Pennell's late, late try.

More Than Survivors
the Rise and Rise of Exeter Chiefs

by STEVE BALE

'Exeter have been eighth, fifth, sixth, eighth and fifth since their promotion. Even the ostensible dip of the season before last had the compensation of victory in the Anglo-Welsh Cup'

W hen Exeter were promoted from the Championship to the Premiership – was it really five years ago? – the question was whether they as a team, a squad and a club would be fit enough to survive. As this has been answered in the affirmative, and increasingly conclusively, in each of the subsequent years, the Chiefs have long since moved on to the next question they posed of themselves at the outset of their elite existence.

PAGE 73 Matt Jess celebrates one of his two tries as the Chiefs thump Sale Sharks 44-16 in the last round of the 2015 Premiership regular season in a bid to reach the last four.

RIGHT Tony Rowe, chairman of Exeter Chiefs, with the LV= Cup during the club's victory parade in April 2014.

FACING PAGE A shrewd acquisition. Thomas Waldrom, who joined Exeter from Leicester in 2014, reaches out to score for the Chiefs against Newcastle in the Challenge Cup. The No. 8 also scored 16 times in the Premiership and was the competition's top try scorer for 2014-15.

Could they, as very few had ever done, join the challengers for Premiership honours? This was a harder task than mere survival but one that Tony Rowe, the club chairman, recognised when he envisaged Exeter turning themselves into a Leicester of the West.

Exeter have done it their own way, but Rowe had taken advice from important people at Welford Road and put a clear progression in place, ambitious but never overambitious and always dependent on the club's successes on and off the field.

As anyone can judge, they are indeed succeeding famously, though finishing fifth as Exeter did last May was actually not a novelty. In 2012, at the end of their second Premiership season, they had missed out on a play-off place only in the last round of the regular season. This season's performance, though, was a long-striding advance over three years previously. Exeter trounced Sale in round 22 but not by enough. Level with Leicester and Saracens, they missed out through having one fewer win than the former and an inferior points difference to the latter. In other words, one more league point would have made them third, not even fourth – the position from which Saracens went through to take the title by winning at Northampton in the semi-final and against Bath in the Twickenham final, so beating first and second.

If Saracens could do this from fourth place, why not Exeter if only it had been them – even allowing for former England manager Geoff Cooke's long-ago assertion that 'if' and 'only' were 'the two most useless words in the English language'? It is going to happen sometime soon enough, because Exeter have a good team who are getting better, a vibrant club getting bigger and – perhaps above all – a lock on the brilliant talent produced on the West Country peninsula.

So Jack Nowell, Henry Slade, Luke Cowan-Dickie and the rest are only the iceberg tip of what Exeter have at their disposal – so much talent, indeed, and such a persistently high standard that much of it inevitably falls by the wayside.

In the Premiership Exeter have been eighth, fifth, sixth, eighth and fifth since their promotion. Even the ostensible dip of the season before last had the compensation of victory in the Anglo-Welsh Cup – a bauble elsewhere, maybe, but at Sandy Park a tremendous achievement.

'You can say it seems scarcely credible what has happened but, being involved in this club and seeing what it has developed into, I can completely see why it's happened. This is no fluke. Hard work is part of it, but there is also ambition.

'Historically the best players in Cornwall and Devon had to go to Bath and Gloucester. Not any more. Now, there's a development pathway for them, at Exeter, to go forward.' This is Dean Mumm speaking, an Australian lock who makes the point just as well.

When Mumm migrated to Devon in 2012 he considered himself definitively an ex-Wallaby. Such was the quality of the rugby he played in assisting Exeter on their upward curve, the Wallabies after all became interested in him again and back he went at the end of our 2014-15 season to Sydney.

Good on him. He was a terrific contributor to Exeter, where the task the revered coach Rob Baxter has set himself is to have more of his wonderful young players attracting the attention of the England head coach Stuart Lancaster.

Tom Johnson and then Nowell were Exeter's first internationals since the 1960s, when wing Martin Underwood won five caps and loose forward Dick Manley appeared throughout the 1963 Five Nations that began with England's last win in Cardiff until 1991. Which is to say Exeter were once a power of sorts in the land, or at least were included in the 'gate-taking clubs' who formed English club rugby's loosely ordered elite in those non-league amateur days. By the time leagues began in 1986 they were good only for the third-tier National Three.

So times have irrevocably changed, ever since the planning gain that got them out of the County Ground and into Sandy Park, touted by Rowe as the biggest conference and banqueting venue in the west of England. Here is one reason Exeter, still unlike most of their Premiership counterparts, run at a profit. Each time they expand their ground – up to 13,000 for the World Cup – it has not been an idle speculation but properly and prudently funded.

It shows how far Baxter's team have come that they were able to give it such a blast against Sale in the final fixture; not dissimilar to how England went about their Six Nations finale against France,

ABOVE Exeter Chiefs' Henry Slade gives Ugo Monye the slip for England against the Barbarians. Slade, along with Luke Cowan-Dickie and established international Jack Nowell, was included in England's training squad for the 2015 World Cup.

FACING PAGE Face of the future? Wing Harrison Cully in action for Chiefs Under 18s on Academy Finals Day 2015 at Allianz Park.

and like England for a few deceptive minutes Exeter looked as if they might even make it.

The coach's particular regret was that Exeter's absence from the semi-finals removed his players from the shop window where Lancaster would be attentively gazing. But whatever regrets Baxter may have had were tempered by the wider realisation of his squad's elevated status.

They were within a few minutes of retaining their Anglo-Welsh title – and this time using far more of a development team than they had in 2013-14 – and also made the semi-finals of the European Rugby Challenge Cup. The ensuing defeat at Gloucester was matched only by their Christmas league defeat at Bath.

'It was a great season having taken some steps forward in our consistency, and the big foundation for that has been our home form, losing two Premiership games, one to Leicester by four points and one to Gloucester by a point,' he said.

'Away from home there was only one game where we didn't take a losing bonus point. We were good enough through the Challenge Cup, reaching the semis, and getting to the LV= Cup final again.

'I know Stuart is very impressed by recent performances and for me the one negative of not pushing through to the top four was that it would have given us another opportunity to showcase a lot of our players.'

To put all of this in context, it is worth reminding ourselves of the fortunes of most of the promoted sides in the 29 years since the Clubs' Championship was launched with Exeter still 24 years from reaching the top flight. Promoted the very first season were Rosslyn Park and Liverpool

St Helens. Rosslyn Park lasted from 1987 to 1991 and have never returned. LSH went straight back down, then straight back up ... and then straight back down again.

West Hartlepool, Rotherham, Rugby, Bedford, London Scottish – for shorter or longer – have all come and gone. Only four – Bath, Gloucester, Leicester and Wasps – of the old first division's original members have never been relegated. Nottingham, Waterloo, Orrell, Coventry, Moseley – between them they are a reminder of how the top end used to be and so of how it has changed. It is also a useful litany of reasons for the assumption that Exeter had every chance of immediately returning in 2011 whence they had come in 2010.

How wrong could people be? Baxter's shrewd annual acquisitions, somehow making up for the holes left even by luminaries such as Mumm, are augmented by the astounding throughput of juniors mentored by Academy Manager Robin Cowling.

Cowling is a former England prop, albeit when playing for Leicester in the late 1970s. He also packed down for Gloucester. He knows what he is talking about and the effectiveness of his system is revealed in how hard it has become to get into it in the first place.

Ultimately it is the Exeter seniors who benefit. Cowan-Dickie, Dave Ewers, Sam Hill, Nowell and Slade are recent graduates with honours. Another group are waiting for their opportunity and three more – Josh Caulfield, Harrison Cully and Jack Maunder – all entered the Exeter Academy in 2015.

'We feel all of them can come through but it's the intermediate stage at the moment,' Cowling said. 'The standard of the club is going up all the time, so it's getting harder and harder for Academy lads to enter.

'Just because they are senior Academy players it doesn't give them a ticket to the first team. It's the bottom rung of the ladder that goes up to the first team. It's a start, not a finish point. Sometimes it can take a little luck but they need to take that luck when it comes.'

There, in a few sentences, you have the secret of Exeter's future success to match the promising present. In Baxter the Chiefs have a chief who always, whether in victory or defeat, says the right thing – impressive in itself – but almost always does the right thing too.

What more do you need? As someone I know rather too well once said, via this very laptop: 'Exeter is not "darkest Devon" but the self-proclaimed capital of the West Country with a rugby plan meticulously drawn up and executed by their own Devonian coach.'

How wise, how prescient.

Sarries' Double: Act I
the LV= Cup

by PAUL BOLTON

'But Exeter were caught offside at a ruck in the final minute and Spencer calmly slotted the resulting penalty to give Saracens the first part of a cup and Premiership double'

There will be no LV= Cup in the 2015-16 season because of the demands placed on clubs by the Rugby World Cup, which is a pity because last season's event, which culminated in a thunderous final, again demonstrated what a valuable competition this has become in developing rugby talent.

Saracens snatched a last-gasp victory over holders Exeter Chiefs in a dramatic final at Northampton's Franklin's Gardens with a nerveless penalty from scrum half Ben Spencer. When Saracens will defend their title and what format the competition might take in the future have yet to be decided, but the uncertainty did not dilute Saracens' jubilation at the final whistle, which came shortly after Spencer had levered over his penalty.

There was plenty of relief in the celebrations for Spencer, who had received the first yellow card of his career in the first half for failing to roll away at a ruck, and also for Saracens who had to dig deep to repel Exeter's superb fightback.

Saracens appeared to be easing to victory when they opened up a 20-6 lead, but Exeter relinquished their title reluctantly. Two converted tries from full back Max Bodilly in an eight-

minute burst levelled the scores and it appeared that extra time would be required to settle a cracking contest. But Exeter were caught offside at a ruck in the final minute and Spencer calmly slotted the resulting penalty to give Saracens their first domestic cup title since they beat Wasps in 1998, and the first part of a cup and Premiership double.

'It was probably the most important kick of my career. I know finals don't come round every day but that is why you practise in those pressure situations. I was glad it went through the middle,' Spencer said.

'That was the first yellow card of my career and it was probably not the best time to get it. But the boys did incredibly well when I was off and when we lost Scott Spurling to the sin-bin which shows what a tightknit group we are.'

The yellow card was the only blemish on an otherwise composed individual display from Spencer who featured prominently in two of his side's three tries. Spencer set up wing David Strettle for his second try with a superb cross-field kick and chipped ahead for flanker Nick de Jager. Strettle's first try came from an interception after he snaffled a ponderous pass from Ben White.

Exeter capitalised when Saracens were again reduced to 14 men by the sin-binning of replacement hooker Spurling as Bodilly crossed twice for tries, both improved by Gareth Steenson. But the Chiefs were left to rue two missed penalty attempts by Ceri Sweeney, one of which struck the crossbar, as Saracens added the Anglo-Welsh Cup to the Premiership A League and Under 18 titles which they had lifted earlier in the season.

Saracens won the LV= Cup mostly with a second-string side who were inspirationally captained by Maro Itoje, the England Under 20 lock, although George Kruis featured as a replacement in the final and in the semi-final victory over Northampton after he was dropped from England's Six Nations squad.

'This win showed what this team has been about all year,' said Saracens' skills coach Joe Shaw. 'This is a special group that never stops fighting and has always found a way.

'We did that again here despite creating a few hurdles for ourselves. I thought that the last ten minutes the way we battled with 14 men to keep going and keep going just shows what this club is all about.'

Despite the disappointment of relinquishing the crown they had won for the first time 12 months earlier, Exeter's assistant coach Ricky Pellow said he was proud of his players.

ABOVE Ben Spencer, scrum half and Mr Reliable with the boot, slots another kick during Saracens' LV= Cup campaign.

FACING PAGE Saracens skipper Maro Itoje hoists the LV= Cup after his side prevailed 23-20 against Exeter in the final at Franklin's Gardens.

'I'm massively proud of the group,' he said. 'As a squad we are disappointed with the way we lost the game. Full credit to Saracens, they put us under a lot of pressure. We did go off script a little bit and, when we did, they punished us.

'That's the sign of a good side. They held on at the end and Ben Spencer, who is a quality kicker, knocked it over. We're going away with a loss and Saracens are moving forward and have an LV= Cup under their belt.'

Once again the competition adopted a confusing playing format, which might have been devised by a chimpanzee with a laptop, in which teams did not play those in the same pool. Teams in Pool One faced those in Pool Four with Pools Two and Three in opposition to ensure that each club had the financial benefit of two home matches.

The final was the sixth successive all-English affair and it was another lean season for the four Welsh regions, who managed just seven wins between them, only five of them against English opposition. Newport Gwent Dragons' 51-35 win at Ospreys was the season's highest score in the competition. Nor did the competition offer London Welsh any comfort away from their struggles at the foot of the Premiership. They lost all four of their group matches, including a 47-7 walloping at Bath in the opening round. But the Exiles came close to an upset against Saracens, who needed two late penalties from the dependable Spencer to eke out a 20-15 win at the Kassam Stadium. London Irish, who propped up Pool Two, were the only other side to go through their cup campaign winless.

Saracens were the only unbeaten side in the competition and one of only two – Leicester were the other – to emerge unbeaten from the pool stage. Saracens' 100 per cent record included a 35-18 win over Exeter at Allianz Park in their final group match, which determined who would have home advantage in the semi-finals.

Exeter topped Pool Four but had to travel to Welford Road in the semi-finals where they outsmarted Leicester in a 30-22 win. Sweeney, the former Wales fly half, kicked half of Exeter's points, but it was a ferocious defensive display and a late try from hooker Greg Bateman that inflicted a first home defeat on Leicester in six months.

FACING PAGE Biyi Alo cannot stop Opeti Fonua from scoring as London Welsh give Sarries a scare at the Kassam Stadium.

BELOW Sebastian de Chaves gathers for Leicester, but visitors Exeter stormed the Tigers' Welford Road fortress to win this semi-final 30-22.

Eastdil Secured

is proud to support

Wooden Spoon Rugby World

EASTDIL
SECURED

A WHOLLY OWNED SUBSIDIARY OF WELLS FARGO & COMPANY

THE REAL ESTATE INVESTMENT BANKING COMPANY

NEW YORK   LOS ANGELES   SAN FRANCISCO   LONDON   CHICAGO
WASHINGTON D.C   ATLANTA   BOSTON   ORANGE COUNTY   RICHMOND
SILICON VALLEY   SAN DIEGO   HONG KONG

Saracens booked their place in the final with a 24-20 win over Northampton in their semi-final at Allianz Park, where a burst of 16 points in the first 15 minutes of the second half proved decisive. In the first half Saracens had made 89 tackles to Northampton's 29, which enabled them to turn round only eight points adrift despite the Saints' apparent superiority. Spencer again demonstrated his value by kicking three penalties, and Mike Ellery, an England Sevens international who had successfully converted to wing from No. 8, scored a superb individual try.

Although England prop Dan Cole made his comeback after nine months out with a neck injury in Leicester's victory over Sale in December, most clubs again used the competition as a development tool. Since all matches were scheduled during the autumn internationals and Six Nations, the cup proved ideal for allowing clubs to blood some of their younger players alongside some older pros in a competition that was a significant step up from A League rugby.

The LV= Breakthrough Player award was won by Northampton's Tom Collins after five weeks of voting by the public. Collins was nominated in November after he scored two tries and assisted in a third in the Saints' 37-23 win over Newcastle Falcons. He also made 18 carries during the match, gained a total of 175 metres in attack and beat seven defenders. By being named LV= Breakthrough Player, Collins followed in the footsteps of England wings Jonny May and Jack Nowell, previous winners of the award. But there will be no opportunity for other youngsters to showcase their talent in a similar way in a World Cup season.

'The likes of Jack Nowell, Henry Slade and Sam Hill cut their teeth in this competition,' Pellow said. 'For our younger guys it'll be a shame that they don't get a chance to have a go at this next year.

'We've got a few younger guys coming in from our academy and that would have been a good tool for them to play in.

'What we will do is pick one or two A League games here and there to get those guys game time.

'The Championship and the guys playing at their loan clubs will also be massively important next season.

'It is a shame because it's a great competition for us as a club. It's going to be disappointing that it's not there next year, but the World Cup will take a big drain in terms of time.'

> **BELOW** Mike Ellery dives in to score a fine individual try for Saracens in their semi-final against Northampton, despite the efforts of LV= Breakthrough Player Tom Collins (No. 11).

SARACENS SPORT FOUNDATION

"Inspiring communities and changing lives through the power of sport"

www.saracens.com/foundation

Allianz Park, Greenlands Lane, Barnet, London, NW4 1RL
Tel: 0203 675 7245 Registered charity no: 1079316

Sarries' Podium Finish
the Aviva Premiership

by CHRIS HEWETT

'Both Saracens and Bath had made statements of their own –
statements so loud, Led Zeppelin themselves would have
struggled to make themselves heard above the din'

It was an American by the name of Eugene W. Baer who gave voice to the notion that 'good
politics is bad economics', adding, for the avoidance of doubt, that 'good economics is bad
politics'. He knew a thing or two. One of the more captivating campaigns in recent Aviva
Premiership history was disrupted, destabilised and ultimately overshadowed by events in the
boardroom – an arena far from the rectangles of mud on which the league positions were decided,
yet at the same time much too close for comfort.

PAGE 79 Champions Sarries get the celebrations under way after their 28-16 victory over Bath in the final at Twickenham.

RIGHT James Wilson makes a break to set up a try for Luther Burrell (right) as Northampton put Gloucester to the sword 53-6 on the opening day of the campaign.

BELOW Ally Hogg and Tom Catterick of the Falcons combine to stop Opeti Fonua of London Welsh. Newcastle finished one rung above bottom-placed Exiles but a massive 33 league points ahead of them.

Two of the three highest-performing sides in the country, Saracens and Bath, contested the grand final at Twickenham, which was only right and proper given the ways in which they had mastered their contrasting brands of rugby. Slightly less satisfying was the fact that both clubs were to be found in the thick of super-sensitive discussions over an inquiry into alleged salary cap abuses. In its infinite wisdom, Premier Rugby eventually decided to suspend a fast-moving investigation into who had been paying what to whom and how, and then attempted to remove the subject from the agenda by refusing to talk about it – a triumph of hope over expectation if ever there was one. At the time of writing, several insiders who had been sworn to secrecy were leaking like sieves.

At the other end of the table, there was the London Welsh issue. The Exiles, promoted unexpectedly at the expense of a cash-rich Bristol, were so hopelessly out of their depth that it was clear by the end of the opening month – some would say the opening weekend – that even a single top-flight win was entirely

beyond them. It was not their fault: having beaten their West Country opponents over two legs of play-off rugby, they had no time to recruit the Premiership-standard personnel they had spent the previous eight months assuming they would not require. All the same, their inability to stack up against the best sides in the country undeniably gave the league a lopsided appearance and quickly breathed fresh life into the dormant debate over the suspension of promotion and relegation. Or, to call a spade a spade, ring-fencing.

Poor old Justin Burnell. The London Welsh coach took heaven's amount of flak for failing to piece together a competitive squad, even though many of his existing players had agreed moves elsewhere and virtually nobody else was available. Burnell failed to survive the season, losing his job in mid-March. By the end of a league programme that heaped Dante-esque misery and indignity on the Exiles, they had registered a Eurovision-style *nul points* while suffering more comprehensive thrashings than a seven-stone swot at a minor public school.

Those Premiership chairmen and chief executives keenest on the idea of expanding the number of clubs in the top division from 12 to 14 and then raising the drawbridge for a period of time – up to five years, according to one enthusiast; a plan eloquently described as a 'prison sentence' by a second-tier Championship coach – insisted it was underpinned by sound financial reasoning. Maybe they had a case, from a pure business perspective. But as the good Mr Baer might have pointed out, there was nothing sound about the politics, as several members of the Rugby Football Union council made abundantly clear. By close of play in May, the battle for hearts and minds was only just beginning.

So to the rugby, which, it was widely rumoured, was the thing that really mattered. At the outset, the reigning champions Northampton were heavily favoured to retain their title, not least because they had not felt the need to add to a squad already eye-wateringly strong. And when they put

ABOVE Jonathan Joseph, the season's outstanding outside centre, goes over during Bath's 45-0 September drubbing of Leicester at the Rec.

FACING PAGE Saracens hooker Jamie George charges home in the 13th minute to score his side's second try of the final at Twickenham. George had recently been called into England's training squad for the World Cup.

50-odd points on Gloucester at Franklin's Gardens in the opening match of the tournament, the odds shortened still further. The visitors had taken the opposite approach to recruitment, bringing in players of exceptional calibre: two Welsh Lions in James Hook and Richard Hibbard, a Scotland captain in Greig Laidlaw, an All Black prop in John Afoa. And a fat lot of good it did them as the likes of George North, Luther Burrell and George Pisi ran riot on the try-scoring front.

Yet before September was out, both Saracens and Bath had made statements of their own – statements so loud, Led Zeppelin themselves would have struggled to make themselves heard above the din. First, the North Londoners spanked Harlequins 39-0 at the Twickenham Stoop. Then, the street-fighting men of Leicester travelled to the Recreation Ground and left on the painful end of a 45-0 monstering. As scorelines go, this was the stuff of fantasy. From here on in, Bath would be the team everyone talked about and wanted to watch.

This had not happened with any consistency since the 'golden decade' on the banks of the River Avon at the end of the amateur era, when the likes of Jeremy Guscott, Stuart Barnes, Richard Hill, Gareth Chilcott, John Hall and Andy Robinson were in their pomp and winning everything under the sun. Later sides, with shackles removed by such imaginative coaches as Brian Ashton and Steve Meehan, hinted at renewal, but could not quite deliver at the decisive moments.

Under the former England defence coach Mike Ford, this latest team played something close to the kind of rugby that had been in Ashton's mind in the mid-noughties: rugby conceived and presented on the broadest of attacking canvases covering the length and breadth of the pitch. The midfielders George Ford, Kyle Eastmond and Jonathan Joseph – the 'holy trinity' – bamboozled opponents with their perfectly timed interplay while the wide players, most notably Anthony Watson and a rejuvenated Matt Banahan, gorged themselves silly on the opportunities presented to them. If whole tables of statistics covering offloads and metres made and defenders beaten failed to register a Bath presence, it was because the Recreation Grounders did things differently by making the ball do the work. Back to the future, you might say.

With Harlequins, another high-tempo attacking side, suffering a downturn in fortunes – partly because of injury, partly because their excellent academy products were not quite excellent enough to deal with the fully fledged international imports ranged against them – only Wasps matched Bath in terms of attacking ambition. Having headed out of London and set up a new base in Coventry, securing their financial future in the process, David Young's side played some exhilarating stuff. Together with the ever-admirable Exeter, who also generated some heat with ball in hand, they might have raced all the way into the play-offs but for a late-season home defeat by Saracens.

Exeter also fell foul of the Londoners, albeit at one remove and even though they registered a famous victory over them in the capital in the penultimate round of matches. Sarries' final game was at London Welsh – a guaranteed landslide – and sure enough, it was points difference that carried them through to the knockout stage at the Devonians' expense.

Those semis were, in their own ways, examples of Premiership rugby at its very best. Saracens travelled to Northampton and prevailed in a bitterly contested, flabbergastingly physical set-to – one in which Dylan Hartley, the Midlanders' combustible hooker and captain, butted his way out of England's training squad for the World Cup by laying his forehead on the cherubic visage of Jamie

George, who, as irony would have it, was promoted to the Red Rose party as a consequence. George deserved it – the call-up, not the assault – for he had been the outstanding No. 2 of the campaign.

Meanwhile, the Bath backs treated Leicester to a second 40-pointer in front of an ecstatic full house at the Rec. If their finishing was nothing short of mesmerising, there was also much to be said for their work without the ball. The Tigers, driven along by the Lions front-rowers Tom Youngs and Dan Cole, had possession aplenty, yet they were repulsed at virtually every turn. Contrary to popular suspicion, the likes of Ford, Eastmond and Joseph proved themselves to be feisty as well as fancy.

Sadly, the showpiece at Twickenham was just a little anticlimactic. Saracens, far more ruthless in generating pressure than Leicester had been, ran away with it in the first half, forcing their opponents into serious errors and scoring three tries as a result. Joseph, the outside centre of the season by a country mile, did conjure a reply after the interval – once again, he looked every inch the 'new Guscott' – but that was the extent of the response. When set against the Sarries-Northampton epic of the previous year, it was a case of 'after the Lord Mayor's Show'.

And in truth, it was a fitting way to end the season. Some of the rugby had been wondrous to behold, but too much had gone on behind the scenes – too much politics, largely driven by economics – to allow the domestic game to feel good about itself. As the old Labour titan Aneurin Bevan once remarked: 'I have never regarded politics as the arena of morals. It is the arena of interests.'

BELOW Twenty-year-old Saracens prodigy Maro Itoje offloads in the tackle during the Premiership final at Twickenham. Itoje captained England Under 20 to the World Championship title in 2014 and also led Saracens to triumph in this year's LV= Cup.

FACING PAGE Charlie Hodgson clocked up another 152 Aviva points in 2014-15, which not only put him top of the Saracens list for the season but maintained his position as the Premiership's all-time leading points scorer with 2469.

Warriors Deliver
the Guinness PRO12

by PETER O'REILLY

'Townsend had a playmaker of substance in 22-year-old Finn Russell, the former stonemason from Stirling, who plays the game with a certain daring, like he's enjoying himself'

Look back to what Gregor Townsend was saying at the launch of the 2014-15 PRO12 and it all makes sense. 'We've now finished fourth, third and second and our goal is to become the first Scottish side to win a title,' said the Glasgow Warriors coach. 'It's something that will drive us this year.'

No one can accuse Townsend of failing to deliver on his objectives. And no one can say the Warriors didn't deserve their success. They were the best-coached side in the Guinness PRO12 and consistently played the most effective, winning rugby. They were good to watch, too – a well-oiled machine but still entertaining, thanks to sublimely skilled individuals like Leone Nakarawa, Mark Bennett and Stuart Hogg.

Critically, Townsend had a playmaker of substance in 22-year-old fly half Finn Russell, the former stonemason from Stirling, who plays the game with a certain daring, like he's enjoying himself – not unlike the way his coach used to do. Russell impressed all season but

BELOW Glasgow Warriors celebrate becoming the first Scottish side to win the PRO12 after beating Munster 31-13 at the Kingspan Stadium, Belfast.

ABOVE Warriors flanker Rob Harley crosses under the posts to score his side's first try of the final in Belfast.

FACING PAGE Denis Hurley touches down for Munster against Ospreys in their semi-final at Thomond Park. The Welsh side almost stole the match at the last, only for the TMO to disallow Josh Matavesi's try for an earlier knock-on.

especially in the PRO12 final, when he guided the Warriors to an emphatic 31-13 victory over Munster in Belfast.

Thus Glasgow became the first Scottish professional side to win a trophy, in 20 years of trying. How they enjoyed it. The lasting image is of the players cavorting with their trophy on the pitch at Kingspan Stadium, while their 4000 travelling supporters repeated their rather obvious but still contagious chant, to the tune of 'Oops Upside Your Head': 'We are Warriors. We are Warriors.'

Having new champions was good for a 14-year-old league that had previously had only four winners: Munster, Leinster, Ulster and Ospreys. Glasgow brought a fresh zest to a tournament that looked in danger a year and a half earlier when the English and French clubs were agitating for a restructuring of European rugby.

As it turned out, that restructuring gave the PRO12 a much-needed shot of adrenalin. By reducing to seven the number of teams that qualified automatically for the new European Champions Cup, the new governing body (EPCR) re-energised the league, to such an extent that the final round of matches in mid-May became another 'Super Saturday', where all six matches had something riding on the result – a place in the play-offs or the possibility of qualifying for the Champions Cup.

Moving the Champions Cup final forward to early May – to placate the French clubs, who wanted a 'clean' run-in for their beloved Top 14 – also worked to the PRO12's advantage. As the weather improved, so too did the spectacle. The league doesn't have the history of the French or English championships, nor does it carry the threat of relegation. But in terms of sporting theatre, this season's run-in compared favourably with the two more established European domestic leagues.

The PRO12 might not have relegation but it did have a casualty of sorts. Leinster failed to make the play-offs for the first time since they were introduced, in 2010, and pretty much as a direct result, their coach, Matt O'Connor, was released with a year still to run on his contract. Various reasons have been offered for O'Connor's sacking, but a primary cause was the pressure created by a more competitive league.

Previously, Leinster had the strength in depth to cope when their internationals were on Six Nations duty – the previous season, they had gathered 19 of a possible 20 points on offer during that window. Last season, opposing teams targeted the champions when they were weak and did so effectively. Harvesting only eight points during February and March ultimately cost O'Connor his job.

The Irish provinces have dominated this tournament in recent years and Munster and Ulster both made the play-offs – unlike Leinster, neither of them qualified from their Champions Cup pool and so it was a little easier to concentrate on the PRO12. Guided by young indigenous coaches Anthony Foley and Neil Doak respectively, Munster and Ulster were rarely out of the top four.

The same can be said of the Ospreys, who led the charge from Wales once again and saved some of their best rugby for the end of the league campaign. I saw them in Galway on that 'Super Saturday', and as Rhys Webb and Dan Biggar ran the show during the first half, they looked odds-on for a bonus-point win and a home semi-final. They didn't nab that bonus and had to play their semi in Limerick. Even then, they were only denied the win by a final-play intervention from the Television Match Official.

The real benefit of the new European system was seen in the performance of Pat Lam's Connacht, who pushed hard for Champions Cup qualification right up to the end but just ran out of steam. If there is one game they will look back on with particular regret, it's their away defeat by Cardiff in February, when they got the wrong end of a couple of critical decisions. Lam was

disciplined for lambasting one of the match officials publicly after the match, but you had sympathy for him and his players.

The standard of officiating remains an issue for the PRO12, as referee managers attempt to get the balance right between blooding young refs and making sure that the best ones get to take charge of the biggest games. Another shortcoming of the competition is the continued weakness of the two Italian franchises, Zebre and Benetton Treviso, who weren't helped by all the political uncertainty in the European game last year and once again finished in the bottom two slots.

LEFT Treviso's Francesco Minto wins line-out ball against Edinburgh at Murrayfield. The Italian teams, Treviso and Zebre, have filled the bottom two PRO12 slots at the end of the past two seasons.

BELOW Scott Williams breaks for the Scarlets as they beat Dragons 29-10 at the Millennium Stadium on Judgement Day. Ospreys defeated the Blues 31-23 in the other leg of the double-header.

Against that, the league's credibility was given a significant boost by attracting a global sponsor in Guinness, and by the arrival of Sky as broadcast partner. Crowds were up significantly on the previous season, boosted by improved attendances at the so-called 'Judgement Days' in Wales – double-headers of local derbies at the Millennium Stadium, branded as quasi-national-trials for Wales coach Warren Gatland.

The PRO12 needs to keep thinking on its feet, as it has stiff competition for players in the shape of both England and, especially, France, where massive television deals mean bigger contracts are on offer – a point recognised by Leinster's chief executive, Mick Dawson.

'I really believe our league needs to have a makeover in terms of brand,' Dawson said in April. 'We also need to attack the UK TV market, because if the Top 14 and the Premiership just keep doing these major TV deals, they'll run away from us. Not only will the clubs have a problem, so will the national teams because we won't be able to hold the players in our territories.

'So, we need the Welsh clubs to make a serious effort to get their players back from France and England. We need to get the Scottish clubs to up their game, particularly Edinburgh.'

The process of self-determination will be helped by the appointment of a dedicated chief executive for next season – up until now, the PRO12 has been just one item on the agenda of John Feehan, who oversees the Six Nations and the British & Irish Lions. Mark Davies, CEO of Pro Rugby Wales, is committed to the idea of a vibrant and commercially thriving PRO12. Like Dawson, he believes the key is in competing with the Premiership in the UK television market.

'There's nearly two and a half million people in England of Celtic birth,' says Davies. 'If you were to take the number that are 25 percent Celtic, it's somewhere between 15 and 20 million people. Add that to the global market place, our position is that we've got more potential growth because of the emotional engagement to those roots.

'The Premiership is better established but there's a greater opportunity for us to escalate, as long as we can be clear what differentiates our product and how it works commercially. That's the exciting thing.

'Nothing's going to be easy but in conversations with the board and among the chief executives, there's a real awakening to the opportunity that exists, a real urgency which is healthy because it's created from competition and the fact that we can't allow the PRL and the Top 14 to go flying away from us.'

The Rugby World Cup will make things difficult for everyone, English and French clubs included, but the PRO12 can only be helped by the return of players like Johnny Sexton and Dan Lydiate from France and the arrival of exciting southern hemisphere backs like All Black Charles Piutau (in Ulster) and Francis Saili, the former Auckland Blue, who has joined Munster.

But now Glasgow are the team to chase. Following that memorable performance in last season's grand final, Townsend spoke about striving to emulate what the Irish provinces have achieved. 'When I played I saw the Irish teams winning trophies and going on to have massive success at pro level,' Townsend said. 'I believe we have had momentum and this trophy will really kick on in terms of what professional sides can do in Scotland.

BELOW Francis Saili on the burst for the Blues against the Rebels in the 2015 Super Rugby competition. Saili has joined Munster for 2015-16.

'We have got to be ambitious as a group to be one of the best sides in Europe and we have played against some top sides. The trophy, while it is fantastic and very satisfying, will also make this team a better team. They have actually gone and delivered and they know what to do when big games come up in the future.'

Toulon Too Good Again
the European Champions Cup

by DAVID HANDS

'To achieve what Toulon have achieved places them in a category of one, even though Leinster won three titles between 2009 and 2012'

Twenty years ago a French club, Toulouse, won the inaugural five-nations European Rugby Cup. Now another French club, Toulon, has won the inaugural European Rugby Champions Cup and, though the game has changed much during the professional era, the same sense of adventure clings to the competition; it has just become that much harder to win.

There have been arguments along the way during what became known as the Heineken Cup (and happily, that particular sponsor remains an integral part of the revamped European tournament). There were no English participants in the opening season, nor in 1998-99 when the English clubs withdrew, but such action was not required during 2014 when both English and French clubs joined forces to insist on merit-based qualification for a 20-strong Champions Cup.

France, with a tier of wealthy backers and salaries unimpeded by so stringent a salary cap as that of England, were best placed to take advantage. Thus it was that two French clubs came together at Twickenham on 2 May when Toulon retained their European crown by beating Clermont Auvergne 24-18 in the final. Indeed France will have more representatives (seven) in the 2015-16 tournament than any other country, thanks to Bordeaux-Bègles claiming the twentieth place by beating Gloucester in the play-off final.

Toulon, moreover, established a European record by registering their third successive victory, having beaten Clermont Auvergne in 2013 and Saracens in 2014. Whether their success has been good for the French national team is an argument to be considered elsewhere, but it is worth remembering the words at the dawn of professionalism of

PAGE 99 Toulon's French international centre Mathieu Bastareaud crashes over just on half-time for his side's first try of the final at Twickenham.

ABOVE Darragh Fanning is unable to catch a flying Christian Wade on his way to the Leinster try line at the RDS. Fanning had the last laugh, though, scoring twice in the home side's 25-20 win.

RIGHT Saints' George North scores his fourth try of the round two clash with Ospreys at Franklin's Gardens, which Northampton won 34-6.

Sir John Hall when he sought to turn Newcastle Falcons into part of a multi-sports empire in the North East.

Sir John, better acquainted with football than rugby, foresaw the day when elite club rugby would become more significant than the international game. How we chuckled when we heard that, but who is to say that, in time, there will not be some truth in it? Toulon, certainly, by buying in so much overseas talent that they started the final with only four Frenchmen, have created something new to rugby which others, if wealthy enough, may emulate.

Certainly they have made themselves the first European club superpower. There will be those who argue that, at different times, Toulouse, Leicester, Wasps, Munster and Leinster have occupied that rarefied atmosphere, but to achieve what Toulon have achieved places them in a category of one, even though Leinster won three titles between 2009 and 2012.

Toulon tripped up only once during the 2014-15 campaign, losing 25-21 to Leicester at Welford Road in a Pool Three match which left a sour taste. Martin Castrogiovanni, the Toulon and Italy prop once the darling of Welford Road, made an extraordinary verbal attack on Richard Cockerill, the Leicester director of rugby, after the match, while during it Delon Armitage, Toulon's full back, addressed abusive language at the home crowd.

Castrogiovanni was subsequently fined and given a suspended four-week ban, but Armitage was banned for 12 weeks, reduced on appeal to eight. Not that it made a vast difference to Toulon, in the happy position of having a Lions full back, Leigh Halfpenny, available after the Welshman's recovery from early-season injuries.

At that stage, midway through the pool matches, it was anyone's guess who would reach the knockout phase. For example, Bath, the rising power in England, lost their first two games: away to Glasgow Warriors, who won by a whopping 37-10, and at home to Toulouse 21-19. Who would predict that they would finish top of Pool Four?

Then there was Northampton, the English champions, denied even a losing bonus point at Racing Métro by on-field mismanagement. Perhaps the most illuminating moment of the first round was the individual try scored for Wasps by Christian Wade during their 25-20 loss to Leinster in Dublin. Throughout the season Wade showed the ability to score tries few other wings could contemplate, yet it was not enough to earn him international selection.

The second weekend brought confirmation that Glasgow's win was not just a flash in the pan. The team that went on to win the Guinness PRO12 title travelled to Montpellier and ground out a 15-13 win thanks to five penalties by Finn Russell, their fly half. Meanwhile Northampton put themselves back on track, with George North scoring four tries in a 34-6 win over the Ospreys.

After the back-to-back rounds of December, only Toulon and Toulouse appeared to be steering clear of danger. Though Clermont Auvergne had become the first French club to win in Munster, they had Saracens on their tail, while Harlequins were in an arm-wrestle with Leinster and Wasps.

But appearances can be deceptive. First to make a move were Wasps, who went to Harlequins and waged so fierce a defensive campaign that, in the first half, they made 112 tackles against 22. They also lost Nathan Hughes to the sin-bin but took every scoring chance that came their way and won 23-3, only to find their effort outshone by Bath.

Jonathan Joseph will look back at the season as a whole fondly enough, but the centre will always remember Toulouse, for the try he created for Francois Louw as well as the one he scored himself in Bath's 35-18 win. It gave Bath a sniff – just a sniff – of a quarter-final and a week later it became a full-blown cold when they beat Glasgow, and Toulouse lost by a point at Montpellier.

That Montpellier win had implications for Saracens too. It meant they had to avoid defeat by 35 points at Clermont to reach the last eight as one of the best pool runners-up, and they duly did so. Wasps gave England their third quarter-finalist (the club's first knockout game in Europe for eight years), while Northampton were the fourth, though they could take little credit after being obliterated 32-8 on their own ground by Racing Métro.

But not one of the English quartet managed a home draw: three had to travel to France and the fourth, Bath, faced a meeting with Leinster, winners in 2009, 2011 and 2012. Bath remained true to their attacking ethos, scored the two tries of the match at the Aviva Stadium and lost 18-15 to six penalties kicked by Ian Madigan.

If this was one that got away from the visitors, Saracens made sure they did not suffer the same fate in Paris. Only ten seconds remained when offside was given against the Racing flanker Fabrice Metz, and the third-choice Saracens goal-kicker stepped forward to try and overturn a two-point deficit. Charlie Hodgson and Alex Goode had already kicked penalties, now Marcelo Bosch lined up a kick from 45 metres, ignored the blustery wind and secured the 12-11 win.

Wasps, who had only qualified for the Champions Cup thanks to the new play-off system, gave Toulon a run for their money at the Stade Mayol before going down 32-18 in a game that Toulon seemed to think was wrapped up at 22-6 before Wasps bounced back. But there was no bouncing back for Northampton at Clermont, who scored four tries in a 37-5 win.

Northampton, missing North because of concussion, were never in the hunt. Noa Nakaitaci scored two tries, Wesley Fofana a third and Nick Abendanon, named player of the tournament the following month, romped 90 metres from turnover ball for the fourth.

This left Saracens with the mighty task of overturning Clermont in a semi-final played in Saint-Etienne, not far from Clermont-Ferrand. A year earlier, at the same stage, Saracens administered a 40-point thrashing to the French side at Twickenham; here they lost 13-9, the decisive blow struck by Fofana, who scored the only try from Brock James's chip kick.

But there were heartening displays from the Vunipola brothers, Mako and Billy, as well as the latest from the Saracens production line, Maro Itoje, on the flank. It was a typically hard-nosed game, which is more than can be said for the other semi-final, played at Marseille between Toulon and Leinster.

It required extra time before Toulon won 25-20 which, given the poor quality of the first 80 minutes, may have been too much for the neutrals in the crowd. But the goal-kicking of Halfpenny,

who scored 20 points, plus an interception try by Bryan Habana saw the champions into the fifth all-French final, played at Twickenham rather than Milan's San Siro, which had been the original choice of the former organising body, European Rugby Cup Ltd.

Whether the Italian ground would have attracted more than the 56,622 who watched the final is a moot point and with no more than a fortnight between semi-finals and final, the expertise of the RFU organisation must have been invaluable. Before the final, European Professional Club Rugby announced that Simon Halliday, the former England centre and subsequently a successful businessman, would chair Europe's governing body, now based in Switzerland.

Another former England international, Jonny Wilkinson, the fly half who had done so much to help Toulon to their pre-eminent position and remained a consultant coach, joined his old colleagues in the build-up to the final. He was a contented man as Toulon won 24-18 despite Clermont taking an 11-3 lead midway through the first half.

Camille Lopez, a replacement at the eleventh hour for James at fly half, gave Clermont the lead with two penalties before Halfpenny responded with the first of four penalties. A charge-down by the arguably offside Morgan Parra gave Fofana the chance to add to his try tally, but before the interval, Mathieu Bastareaud barrelled over after Toulon ran back ball kicked to them by Abendanon.

Halfpenny's kicking pushed Toulon into an eight-point lead in the third quarter, but Abendanon collected a poor clearance from Habana, ran, chipped and collected himself to score the try which, with Lopez's conversion, reduced the margin to one. It took a moment of magic from Drew Mitchell, Toulon's Australian wing, to make the result certain when he took off on a short-side run some 40 metres from the line and beat six defenders en route to a try. It was a fine end to a fine match and a masterful season for Toulon.

LEFT Coup de grâce at HQ. Clermont having got back to within a point through a superb individual try from Nick Abendanon, Toulon replied with this Drew Mitchell special. Here the Australian passes Abendanon just prior to crossing the line.

Gloucester's Glory
the European Challenge Cup
by HUGH GODWIN

'Jonny May sprinted on a line deep behind Twelvetrees' decoy dart. Twelvetrees followed up in support to finish the try from May's pass out of the tackle'

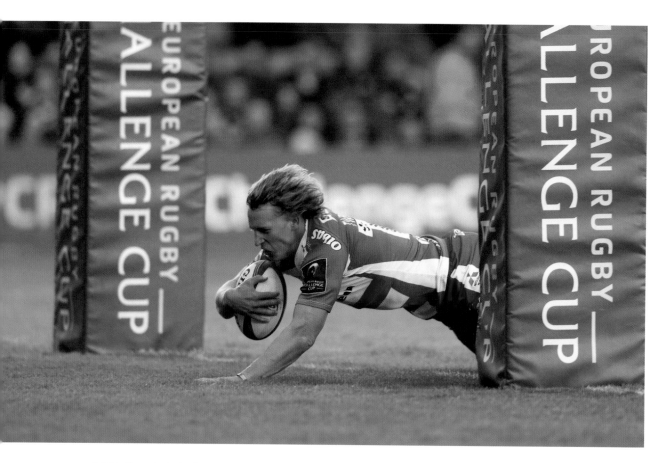

The night before the all-French final of the European Rugby Champions Cup at Twickenham, the spotlight fell on Harlequins' Stoop stadium across the road, and an Anglo-Scottish joust for the junior partner to the main event: the Challenge Cup.

Edinburgh had been plonked into the second-tier competition by the change in format that reduced the number of teams in the Champions Cup from 24 to 20, as well as a cut in Scotland's automatic places from two to one (taken by Glasgow). It was a demotion but also an opportunity, and Edinburgh breezed past Lyon, Bordeaux-Bègles and London Welsh in their Challenge Cup pool and London Irish and Newport Gwent Dragons in the knockout rounds to reach a first European final for any Scottish team. By contrast, Gloucester had form over course and distance, having won the Challenge Cup at the Stoop in 2006, beating London Irish 36-34 in extra time. They knew a disappointing league season – ninth place in the Premiership, despite much hope vested in a new coaching staff led by David Humphreys and Laurie Fisher – would be rescued to a degree by winning this trophy. The aim was to complete a clean sweep of wins in the campaign, after Oyonnax, Zebre, Brive, Connacht and Exeter Chiefs had been knocked over along the way. Gloucester's excited supporters queued up at Kingsholm at 7.30am the day tickets went on sale, and the M4 to London was a busy motorway on Friday 1 May.

Gloucester had a bigger pack, and in the absence of the injured back-rowers Ben Morgan and Sione Kalamafoni, they were expected to deploy the likes of Ross Moriarty – the son of the former Wales flanker Paul – to carry the ball hard around the corner of rucks. Edinburgh's team sheet was sprinkled with names like Du Preez, Strauss, Nel and Bresler as evidence of the southern African influence in the team – the so-called 'Jock Boks' – engineered by the Scottish Rugby Union and guided by the head coach Alan Solomons, who hails from the Eastern Cape. At scrum half, Gloucester's Scotland captain Greig Laidlaw went head-to-head with his international understudy, Sam Hidalgo-Clyne, whose five Test caps in 2015 were a big step from being fourth choice Edinburgh No. 9 in 2014. The year before that, he had been a reluctant convert from fly half.

Hidalgo-Clyne's penalty goal prodded Edinburgh ahead after two minutes, but it was soon equalised by Laidlaw, who had been Edinburgh's captain under Solomons before moving to Kingsholm. And the remainder of the first half was mostly a tale of Gloucester attack

FACING PAGE Skipper Billy Twelvetrees scores for Gloucester in the 11th minute of the final at the Stoop.

BELOW Cornell Du Preez tap-tackles Jonny May to stop him extending Gloucester's lead.

against Edinburgh defence. Adventurous handling by the Cherry and Whites' James Hook and Billy Twelvetrees – the fly half and inside centre playing flat to the gain line – stretched their black-shirted opponents this way and that, although the only time Edinburgh cracked was with a single-phase try in the 11th minute. A two-handed catch by Tom Palmer at a line out near the halfway line allowed Laidlaw and Hook to launch a smooth set-piece move, with Jonny May sprinting on a line deep behind Twelvetrees' decoy dart. Twelvetrees followed up in support to finish the try from May's pass out of the tackle.

Laidlaw's conversion put Gloucester 10-3 up and they looked confident. When Edinburgh's New Zealander centre Sam Beard lost possession in the Gloucester half, May countered with a thrilling run that took him very close to a second try of the evening, only for Cornell Du Preez to thwart him with a fingertip tap-tackle. With his socks rolled down, a long-legged gait reminiscent of an 800-metre runner, and a slightly madcap approach to his thoughts and deeds, May is one of rugby's most glorious if unpredictable sights on the hoof.

During the same spell of intense pressure, Gloucester wasted chances to increase their lead: Gareth Evans – the No. 8 in Morgan's absence – was held up over the goal line, Edinburgh's Namibian lock Anton Bresler went to the sin-bin, and the resulting five-metre scrum yielded Gloucester a penalty and free kick but no points as the third scrummage ended with John Afoa penalised for collapsing. It was one of those occasions when you wondered why a tight-head prop in an attacking position would do such a thing, but the French referee Jérôme Garcès had no doubt. Maybe it was one up for Al Dickinson, the Edinburgh loose-head once of Gloucester.

Much relieved, though still a man short, Edinburgh put together a multiphase move of their own, and collected a penalty goal by Hidalgo-Clyne, though the scrum half would go on to miss a kick in the last act before the interval. In between, Laidlaw's second penalty – for Edinburgh sealing off – had Gloucester 13-6 up but surely thinking it should have been more.

Better to be ahead than behind, nevertheless, and in an eventful and controversial second half, Edinburgh were unable to haul Gloucester in. The English club's ascendancy was confirmed by Richard Hibbard's strong carry and a grubber by centre Billy Meakes very nearly collected for a try by Charlie Sharples, followed by two penalties for ruck offences kicked by Laidlaw in the 50th and 54th minutes: 19-6.

Then, a wobble. A rare break by Edinburgh's expert try poacher Tim Visser, though fruitless in itself, had originated at a messy scrum on halfway which replays showed had concluded with Moriarty dropping a knee into Fraser McKenzie's back. Moriarty was shown a yellow card, later upgraded to a two-week suspension after a citing.

Obviously, it was imperative Edinburgh made the most of the next ten minutes. In fact, this was just the start of a thoroughly awkward finish for Gloucester, shaped initially by lapses in discipline, but eventually rescued by stubborn teamwork. Awarded a penalty close to the Gloucester goal line, Edinburgh went for the line out, but while the catch was safe, a fumble in the subsequent drive undid them – a tribute to the defensive burrowing of Evans, Afoa and others. Next, in a reprise of Gloucester's first-half frustration in the same spot on the field, Edinburgh and Dickinson were aghast to see the ensuing scrum end in a penalty to the defending team.

Now Laidlaw, Hook and Twelvetrees put boot to ball, aiming to spend as much of the sin-bin period as possible in Edinburgh territory. Phil Burleigh, the Edinburgh fly half, had already suffered a couple of inaccurate restarts, and he appeared uncertain how to deal with the aerial threat. He was happier on the run from a line out, and although Edinburgh lost their way at the corner again, as with the Moriarty incident, the referee's whistle signalled a review of Gloucester foul play. Meakes had responded to Beard running at him on a decoy line by grabbing his opponent momentarily around the neck. The television match official Eric Gauzins recommended a red card and Garcès complied. Twelvetrees, the Gloucester captain, argued unsuccessfully that Beard had been in front of the ball, off Meakes went – eventually to be banned, like Moriarty, for two weeks – and Gloucester

were reduced to 13 men for the next minute and a half, and 14 men for the remaining 15 minutes after that.

From a series of rucks in the Gloucester 22, hooker and former Scotland captain Ross Ford reached through Evans' tackle to score a try for Edinburgh, converted by Hidalgo-Clyne. The points margin was down to six, and the earlier snazziness of Gloucester's running was replaced by hard graft and scrambling tackles. Moriarty returned to the field, Meakes was shown in television close-ups apparently shedding tears, and the thousands of Gloucester 'Shed Heads' in the crowd gulped a deep breath or a restorative beer, or both. Afoa and Hibbard, signed at great expense the previous summer, were pinged for a fifth penalty of the final in the scrum. But Edinburgh's handling and kicking and discipline at the breakdown were just not accurate enough and the time slipped by with no further scoring. Umpteen rucks navigated with admirable composure by Gloucester, and a penalty shot by Laidlaw that went dead behind the posts, heralded the final whistle.

May, the man of the match, said: 'Having been at Gloucester for so long, with my mates, makes this a night I'll remember for the rest of my life.' Twelvetrees hailed the 'incredibly hard work' of a much-changed group of players and coaches. Mike Coman, Edinburgh's skipper and former Hawke's Bay flanker, said: 'We had opportunities in that second half but coughed them up. Congratulations to Gloucester: they turned up and we didn't slow their ball down enough at the breakdown.'

The 19-13 win gave Gloucester not only a welcome second European trophy after a nine-year wait but also entry into the end-of-season play-off series for the twentieth and last Champions Cup place for 2015-16. They overcame Connacht from the PRO12, 40-32 after extra time, at Kingsholm but then lost to the French Top 14's seventh-placed club, Bordeaux-Bègles, 23-22, in a match played at Worcester because Kingsholm was unavailable. So, Gloucester will play in the Challenge Cup again in 2015-16 – in a pool alongside Worcester, as it happens – and it felt about right as the measure of a season in transition, while Edinburgh were left to ponder whether their southern-hemisphere signings were taking them in the right direction.

LEFT Billy Twelvetrees and Gloucester lift the European Rugby Challenge Cup after a tense finish to the final at the Stoop.

next

ARE HAPPY TO SUPPORT THE

THE WOODEN SPOON

REVIEW OF THE SEASON 2014-15

Ireland's on Points
the RBS 6 Nations Championship
by CHRIS JONES

'Yes, the 2015 championship provided the kind of climax you could not have predicted, but it still seems unfair that teams going into their matches were able to tailor their tactics'

I reland retained the RBS 6 Nations title at the end of the most dramatic final day the championship has ever staged. First Wales put themselves in pole position, after the earliest of the staggered kick-offs, beating Italy 61-20 in Rome, and then Ireland set the new benchmark by accounting for Scotland 40-10 at Murrayfield, which left England needing to beat France at Twickenham by 26 points. They came up six points short after an amazing 55-35 victory.

ABOVE Ireland's Sean O'Brien scores the late try in Edinburgh that, with Ian Madigan's conversion, meant England had to win by 26 at Twickenham.

Twelve months earlier, Ireland played last and won 22-20 against France in Paris to take the title while England watched the game in Italy; they had earlier hammered their hosts 52-11, only to discover it was not enough. In 2015 it was England who had the advantage of knowing what they needed to do, but still they could not repeat their 2011 title success.

Despite the heart-stopping moments that made the day so memorable, I still do not agree with staggered kicks-off on the final day of the tournament. Yes, the 2015 championship provided the kind of climax you could not have predicted, but it still seems unfair that teams going into their matches were able to tailor their tactics to try and meet a known criterion for success.

England had a real advantage, as they were able to sit back and watch the other two matches; and yet they still fell short because while trying to record the required 26-point winning margin, Robshaw's men forgot that they also had to stop the French from scoring. That meant that despite 55 points in their favour (a truly staggering total given they were playing France) England lost out due to the 35 they conceded.

So how did that mad, mad final Saturday unfold?

England started the day as leaders from Ireland on points difference, with Wales some way back and hardly warranting a mention in how the title mix would be sorted out.

That view appeared to be correct as Warren Gatland's Wales team led Italy by only a point at half-time in Rome but suddenly produced their best in the second half, with George North's hat-trick ensuring Ireland needed to beat Scotland by 21 points to take the lead on points difference.

Scotland, who ended up winless and with the Wooden Spoon despite the arrival of new coach Vern Cotter, could not stop the Irish from earning a 30-point winning margin, which immediately ruled Wales out of title contention and set England that daunting 26-point target against the unpredictable French (when are they anything different!).

In a match that generated 12 tries – one by George Ford, who amassed 25 points on his own – England pulled clear but never managed to get into a lead that would have denied Ireland the title. Jack Nowell's try with five minutes remaining put them 20 points ahead, and the players and the crowd knew that a converted try would have given England the championship. However, this was a game that England did not control with the kind of killer instinct you felt the All Blacks would have brought to the table, and the sin-binning of James Haskell for a needless trip summed up their lack of poise in crucial moments. It left Ireland to head into the Rugby World Cup as Europe's champion country for a second successive year and England branded the nearly men again. The means to win the close matches is something the best teams develop and there remained a real concern that even as World Cup hosts, England would rue two years of missed chances to prove the doubters wrong.

It had all started so well for head coach Stuart Lancaster in Cardiff where England emerged 21-16 winners against Wales, who appeared to still be lacking a Plan B once the opposition had stopped their famed power game, which comes under the title 'Warrenball' in honour of the Wales and Lions coach. England's win was even more impressive, as they had been forced to make five changes from the starting XV that defeated Australia 26-17 at Twickenham in November. Brad Barritt, Dave Wilson, Courtney Lawes, Tom Wood and Ben Morgan were ruled out of selection by injury; Owen Farrell and Joe Launchbury were also absent injured. Into the starting line-up came centres Jonathan Joseph of Bath and Luther Burrell of Northampton (with Billy Twelvetrees moved to the replacements' bench), prop Dan Cole (Leicester), lock George Kruis (Saracens), flanker James Haskell (Wasps) and No. 8 Billy Vunipola (Saracens).

FACING PAGE Jonathan Joseph opens his Six Nations account, dancing past the Wales defence to touch down in Cardiff.

BELOW Replacement Dougie Fife scores the only try of Scotland's match in Paris just before half-time. The visitors, though, were undone by five penalties from French fly half Camille Lopez.

ABOVE The Italians celebrate at no-side at Murrayfield after snatching victory through a 79th-minute penalty try.

FACING PAGE Lock Yoann Maestri scores France's first try as they defeat Italy 29-0 in Rome during the penultimate round of matches.

The England replacements included 36-year-old former captain Nick Easter (Harlequins), making his first appearance in the Test squad since the 2011 Rugby World Cup, while Sale outside half Danny Cipriani had not featured since 2008. England showed that if you can hold out against the power game, then Wales could be beaten.

Italy had high hopes going into their opening game against champions Ireland but ended up losing 26-3 to start what would be another topsy-turvy season, only brightened by the 22-19 away win over Scotland in the third round of matches. That loss saw the glass door in the Scotland coaches' box left with a large impact smash, which just about completed a terrible day for the eventual Wooden Spoon winners.

It had looked so different for the Scots, who only lost 15-8 to Camille Lopez's five penalties first up in Paris against a French side that would, yet again, flatter to deceive in what was coach Philippe Saint-André's final championship in charge of his men. France had Ireland in all sorts of trouble in Dublin before the Irish emerged 18-11 winners, with Johnny Sexton kicking five penalties and Ian Madigan one; this would turn out to be a critical victory in their bid to retain the title.

England built on their Cardiff win by accounting for Italy 47-17 in a match that would have a dramatic effect on full back Mike Brown's season. The Harlequins player made a typically brave tackle on Italy and Wasps back Andrea Masi, only for his head to connect with the opposition player's shoulder. Brown went off concussed, returned having passed the relevant protocols, but then suffered a reaction and did not play again for the rest of the season due to headaches. Concussion and its treatment was to be a major feature of the domestic and international season, and Brown highlighted just how much care must be taken with players who suffer head knocks.

Scotland seemed to have found a real competitive edge as they appeared to be ready to turn over Wales at Murrayfield before the visitors further deflated home supporters with a 26-23 win. Centre Jonathan Davies scored the crucial try on the hour mark for Wales, with Jon Welsh's try coming too late for the Scots.

The feelings of disappointment in the home dressing room at Murrayfield at the end of their next game against Italy were in stark contrast to those in the one housing the elated Azzurri. While they have beaten the Scots before, an away win is still something to savour for the Italians, who had scored three tries to Scotland's one. Greig Laidlaw's accuracy with the boot had looked set to ensure a home win. However, referee George Clancy did not hesitate to award a last-gasp penalty try and Tommaso Allan's conversion was the icing on the cake as Italy secured only their second away win in the Six Nations.

The Parisian crowd showed their anger as Dan Biggar's second-half try and the boot of Leigh Halfpenny brought Wales a fourth successive win over France, 20-13, to keep them in the title hunt, while England's Grand Slam hopes came crashing down around them

yet again in Dublin where the Irish were deserved 19-9 winners. England's points came from George Ford's boot, and the Bath youngster was proving to be more than just a stand-in for the injured Owen Farrell; this would be a championship to show he could be the first choice, even when his former schoolmate was fit again.

By the penultimate round of games, it seemed it was the Irish who would claim the Slam, although their fans knew that nothing could be taken for granted in Cardiff. Sure enough, Wales ruined Irish dreams of a Slam with a 23-16 win. Five Halfpenny penalties and a crucial try by replacement Scott Williams helped negate the yellow cards for Jonathan Davies and Sam Warburton in a defensive performance that had coach Shaun Edwards purring with delight. It was Paul O'Connell's 100th cap – but not Ireland's day.

Tries from Jonathan Joseph, George Ford and Jack Nowell put England in command when they faced Scotland, but the excellent Mark Bennett replied for the visitors, who managed to stop Stuart Lancaster's men from romping away; the 25-13 result would prove to be crucial as points difference eventually settled the title that amazing final Saturday. France headed to Rome and proved they could play some rugby by recording a 29-0 win featuring second-half tries from Yoann Maestri and Mathieu Bastareaud, with the Italian season further deflated by that 60-point final round beating by Wales at the end of a truly amazing championship.

FACING PAGE Led by Paul O'Connell in his 100th appearance for his country, Ireland drive desperately for the line in the dying moments at Cardiff. Wales held out defiantly to halt Ireland's Grand Slam bid.

BELOW England's seventh try against France, courtesy of Jack Nowell and duly converted by George Ford, put England 20 points clear with five minutes left, but they could not conjure another score.

HEAVE!

The Club Scene
England: Déjà Vu for Bristol

by NEALE HARVEY

'And yet disaster struck again when, having broken clear to lead Worcester 58-45 on aggregate with just eight minutes remaining, Robinson's side managed to chuck away the game'

Bristol appear to have perfected the art of failing to win promotion and, sadly for them, their generous benefactor Steve Lansdown and some incredibly loyal supporters, who flocked to the club's new Ashton Gate home in huge numbers to watch an all-star team containing such luminaries as Dwayne Peel, Gavin Henson, Matthew Morgan and Ryan Jones, Andy Robinson's side again fluffed their lines at the vital moment, somehow conjuring a defeat of mind-numbing proportions from the jaws of victory in a dramatic two-legged Greene King IPA Championship final against Worcester.

Bristol having left their spiritual home at the Memorial Ground to ground-share with Bristol City, with both clubs coming under the auspices of Lansdown's innovative Bristol Sport concept, this was the season when they really needed to go up. A seventh year in the second tier could not be contemplated by a club that was spending £45 million on redeveloping Ashton Gate into a 27,000-capacity facility and has bold ambitions of challenging the best teams in the Aviva Premiership and, eventually, Europe.

And yet disaster struck again when, having broken clear to lead Worcester 58-45 on aggregate with just eight minutes of the second leg at Sixways remaining, Robinson's side managed to chuck away the game and, with it, their season. The Championship play-off concept has its critics, and rightly so, but Bristol only have themselves to blame and must now go back to the drawing board.

In the meantime, after losing £2.5 million in 2013-14, the financial losses will continue to

RIGHT Worcester Warriors celebrate their return to the top flight of English rugby, having consigned Bristol to at least one more season in the Championship after a sensational final few minutes of the play-off second leg at Sixways.

mount for Bristol, with their devastated chairman Chris Booy reflecting: 'Clearly we will lose a lot of money next season. We'd love to control our losses at £2.5 million but it'll be worse this year and we'll still be investing to get back into the Premiership, so in 2015-16 we'll be taking another big hit.

'Our strategy is to get into the Premiership and we believe we can get the necessary crowds and sponsors to be able to compete at the top and generate more money in future. For a club of our scale, we simply can't continue to play in the Championship. Andy Robinson's brief is very clear now, we have to win promotion next year. We've got a fantastic fan base who can see a great future for the club and, believe me, it will happen. I'll go as far as staking my reputation on it.'

While Bristol indulged in their annual bout of navel-gazing, disaster also struck further west where once-mighty Plymouth almost went into administration before being relegated. After briefly flirting with promotion around the mid-noughties, the Brickfields outfit fell into steep decline and finances have been stretched. Relegation at least provides an opportunity to regroup and rebuild on and off the field, but their rugby director, former England hooker Graham Dawe, faces a huge task to win promotion from a highly competitive National One with what amounts to a new side.

Elsewhere in the GKIPA Championship, London Scottish's heartwarming renaissance continued apace as they finished third, their highest league position since the club re-formed in 2000, to make the play-offs for the first time, where they were defeated by eventual champions Worcester. Rotherham reached the play-offs for a second successive year under head coach Lee Blackett, who has since headed to Wasps, while Nottingham belied budget limitations to finish a creditable fifth.

Jersey, a growing force in the game, made progress to end up seventh, while promoted side Doncaster comfortably stayed up, along with Moseley who celebrated their survival by opening a new £3.4-million grandstand aimed at putting the West Midlands side on a firmer financial footing. Increased funding for Championship clubs this season, along with the possibility of a new television deal with BT Sport, ought to ensure English rugby's second tier goes from strength to strength.

Meanwhile Worcester completed a league and British & Irish Cup double, their impressive second-string side comfortably beating Doncaster 35-5 in a one-sided final at Castle Park. It was due reward for their estimable captain in the competition, Jean-Baptiste Bruzulier, who later demonstrated his value by coming to the Warriors' rescue in the Championship final against Bristol when both the club's senior scrum halves were ruled out.

FACING PAGE The referee's whistle brings the final of the Bill Beaumont Cup to an end, and this year it is Cornwall who are victorious, having beaten Lancashire 18-13.

BELOW Jamie Broadley of Rotherham Titans scores against Bristol in the Championship play-off semi-final second leg at Abbeydale.

Ealing Trailfinders bounced back into the Championship at the first attempt by edging a compelling National One title race that saw them, Rosslyn Park and a revitalised Coventry slugging it out. Trailfinders, heavily backed by travel industry magnate Mike Gooley, joined Saracens and Newcastle by installing a 4G artificial grass pitch and the move paid off handsomely; Rosslyn Park are now following suit. For their part, Coventry will be pushing hard for promotion once again this time around.

Fylde continue to impress, while two sides worth keeping an eye on this season are Hartpury College, a growing force in the west who are benefiting from close ties with Premiership outfit Gloucester, and Darlington Mowden Park, who purchased the hugely impressive 25,000-capacity Northern Echo Arena three years ago and have ambitions of becoming fully professional. It's early days, but look out for them providing serious opposition to Newcastle Falcons in future.

There was drama at the bottom of National One as the relegation battle went down to the wire, largely as a result of a faux pas by Old Albanians, who were deducted five points due to a player registration error. That offered a lifeline to Cinderford, who promptly reeled off four successive bonus-point victories to stay up. Tynedale and Macclesfield joined Old Albanians in falling through the trapdoor, but the latter will be confident of promotion under new coach James Shanahan.

The National Two North title race was dominated by Hull Ionians and Ampthill, with the Yorkshire side eventually prevailing. Ampthill, who are coached by former Wales centre Paul Turner, were consigned to a play-off against Bishop's Stortford, who ended the season as runners-up to champions Henley Hawks in National Two South. A record crowd of over 2000 turned up at Ampthill to watch the village side win 19-10 and earn a place amongst the nation's top 40 clubs for the first time – quite an achievement for a place that boasts a population of fewer than 6000!

Hull, Birmingham & Solihull and Stockport dropped out of National Two North, while Lydney, Shelford and Bristol outfit Dings Crusaders were the patsies in National Two South. They will be replaced by Bury St Edmunds, Redingensians, Sale and South Leicester, who were champions of their respective National Three divisions, along with Barnes and Sandal who were promoted via the play-offs. South Leicester were the best of the bunch, winning the Midlands league by 24 points.

Elsewhere, the little-reported-on County Championship, nowadays known as the Bill Beaumont Cup, continued its welcome revival as Cornwall claimed their first title since 1999 with a thrilling 18-13 win over Lancashire. Over 3000 Cornish fans made the long journey to Twickenham for the noon kick-off, offering conclusive proof that the County Championship – seen as an anachronism by some – still has a place in the game. Surrey took home the County Plate with a 17-3 victory over the Eastern Counties, while Leicestershire claimed the County Shield by beating Cumbria 34-17.

Lower-league cup competitions again proved popular and it was Maidstone who claimed the honours in the RFU Intermediate Cup with a 31-18 win over Bridgnorth, while Bromley ensured a Kent double by beating West Leeds 16-10 in the RFU Senior Vase and the wonderfully monikered Battersea Ironsides added the RFU Junior Vase to their Surrey One title with a 30-15 victory over 2013-14 Vase winners Longlevens. They were dancing in the streets of Battersea that night!

Scotland: Glasgow All the Way

by ALAN LORIMER

'They say that inside every Fijian lock forward there is a centre and at Kingspan Nakarawa proved the point, running, sidestepping and passing like a top threequarter'

At last. The long wait is finally over after Glasgow Warriors won the Guinness PRO12 title, ending years of wondering if a Scottish club would ever achieve major honours. Warriors did so and with the double satisfaction of finishing top of the Guinness PRO12 league and then confirming their primacy by winning the play-off.

Glasgow Warriors had reached the play-off final in the previous season only to be well beaten by Leinster in Dublin. Twelve months later on neutral soil at the Kingspan Stadium in Belfast, Warriors put on a show of running rugby that demolished Munster's hopes of reclaiming the top position among the Celtic and Italian clubs.

It was a performance that showcased Glasgow's attractive style, an adventurous approach to rugby, instilled into the club by Warriors' inspirational mentor, Gregor Townsend, deservedly named as the Guinness PRO12 coach of the season.

The former British & Irish Lions fly half had built up a squad of players suited to the kind of fast, attacking rugby he espoused. Townsend, also capped 82 times by Scotland, had been astute in signing two remarkable Fijians, scrum half/wing Niko Matawalu and lock/back-row Leone Nakarawa, who both were key to realising the coach's vision of the way his side should play.

Matawalu had become something of a cult hero at Glasgow's Scotstoun ground, the Fijian maestro accumulating a string of man-of-the-match awards in his seasons with the Warriors. But in the final it was the athletic Nakarawa who provided the stellar performance.

They say that inside every Fijian lock forward there is a centre and at Kingspan Nakarawa proved the point, running, sidestepping and passing like a top threequarter to create tries for flanker Rob Harley and winger DTH van der Merwe in early assaults on the Munster line. With both tries converted by Finn Russell, Glasgow were well on their way to victory, and when Stuart Hogg laid on the scoring pass for scrum half Henry Pyrgos it was practically all over for Munster.

It certainly was when Finn Russell converted his own second-half try, and thereafter the celebrations could begin. On 67 minutes Glasgow's long-serving club captain Alastair Kellock came off the bench to tumultuous applause in his valedictory appearance for Warriors. It was a poignant moment and the perfect send-off for the big Glaswegian. Matawalu, too, came off the bench in his last game for the club to soak up the acclaim of the Glasgow fans at the Belfast ground.

It had been a perfect performance by Glasgow and one that was very much Townsend. Perhaps too it was about the relief at having reached the final after a tense semi at Scotstoun in which Glasgow had been second best to Ulster for most of the game. But going into the final minutes of the match and trailing 14-9, Glasgow worked their way through several phases before Russell threw a long pass to van der Merwe for the wing to cross in the corner and level the scores at 14-14. Russell then held his nerve, kicking the winning conversion goal from the touch line for a 16-14 victory.

Russell was one of Glasgow's young stars in their Guinness PRO12 campaign, but there were massive contributions, too, from centres

FACING PAGE After falling at the final hurdle in 2013-14, Glasgow Warriors are PRO12 champions at last in Belfast.

BELOW Niko Matawalu, one of a pair of outstanding Fijians at Scotstoun, beats Dan Evans during Glasgow's home PRO12 match against Ospreys.

Peter Horne and Richie Vernon, who took over from the first-choice midfield pairing of Alex Dunbar and Mark Bennett following Six Nations injuries to the Scotland duo. Then of course there were telling performances from the irrepressible Hogg and wingers Tommy Seymour and van der Merwe and scrum half Pyrgos. Among the forwards Josh Strauss was immense, as was Harley, Jonny Gray and Doug Hall, the latter making sure he retired from professional rugby on a high.

If Glasgow had excelled in the Guinness PRO12, then when it came to European rugby the Scotstoun club fell just short. A decisive win over Bath at the beginning of the competition raised hopes, but after defeating Montpellier twice and losing to Toulouse home and away Warriors lost out narrowly to Bath in the final pool match and thus failed to reach the knockout stages.

Fifty miles to the east, Edinburgh Rugby enjoyed a good campaign in the European Challenge Cup, finishing top of their group – containing Bordeaux-Bègles, Lyon, and London Welsh – to book a place in the quarter-finals, where they achieved an away win against London Irish.

Then in the semis Edinburgh swept aside Newport Gwent Dragons to win 45-16, but in the final at the Stoop, the Scottish capital side paid for a slow start against Gloucester, who claimed the title with a 19-13 win, 14 of the winners' points coming from the former Edinburgh skipper Greig Laidlaw.

Edinburgh had shown encouraging form in European rugby, but in the Guinness PRO12 it was another disappointing season for the Murrayfield outfit, who finished eighth; their coach, Alan Solomons, had to deflect widespread criticism of fielding too many foreign players.

But Solomons, by taking a gamble on young talent, at least accelerated the international careers of scrum half Sam Hidalgo-Clyne, flanker Hamish Watson and lock Ben Toolis. The clamour for Edinburgh to use more Scotland players will continue and in that context Solomons has in his squad the likes of Damien Hoyland, who benefited from a stint with the national Sevens squad and enjoyed a hat-trick of tries against England at Twickenham, and Ben Robbins, a former New Year Sprint winner – two wingers either of whom could fill the vacancy created by the departure of Scotland cap Tim Visser.

Meanwhile, Edinburgh had another season condemned to play in the inappropriately large 67,500-seater stadium that is Murrayfield when their crowd numbers averaged around 4000. It has become a perennial problem for Edinburgh and a solution remains elusive. Rumours that Edinburgh might use Easter Road, the home of Hibs FC, raised hopes of a possible move, but talks between the two clubs suggest it might be a long wait before any deal can be struck.

Glasgow and Edinburgh together represent the sum total of professional rugby north of the border, a precariously small base of professional players and inadequate to support a national team. What is desperately needed is a third professional team (and indeed a fourth), but thus far Scottish Rugby has insisted that finances are simply not there for such an expansion.

In the absence of further professional teams being created, there is a plan to make the top layer of the amateur game, the Premiership, semi-professional and to make it an eight-team league. The idea is to concentrate the talent in a small number of teams and make the Premiership an effective interface between the amateur and professional games.

Certainly there is evidence that standards in the Premiership are ever increasing and in doing so are contributing to a product that is popular with players and spectators alike. In the 2014-15 season, competition was intense, with both title and relegation issues going to the wire. In the event Heriot's celebrated their 125th anniversary year by finishing top of the league ahead of Ayr, Melrose and Gala before going on to win the inaugural play-off competition with a narrow win over Melrose.

Heriot's fully deserved their title honours after complementing hard forward play with exciting running from their backs. Heriot's, however, were thwarted by Hawick in their attempt to achieve a league/cup double after losing to the famous Border club in the semi-finals. But Hawick's hopes of winning the cup were crushed by a Boroughmuir side which saved its best display of the season to overrun the Greens.

Relegated this season were Edinburgh Accies, whose place in the Premiership was taken by the National League winners, Selkirk, meaning that for the 2015-16 campaign, there are four Border clubs in the top flight, joining three from Edinburgh, two from the west and one from Caledonia. 'Amateur' clubs are vibrant, and with innovative support from Murrayfield following an inflow of funds as a consequence of Scottish Rugby's deal with telecoms giant BT, they will almost certainly play a greater role in the production of professional players. Exciting times, it seems, lie ahead for the club scene in Scotland.

Wales: The Hour Before the Dawn?

by DAVID STEWART

'The Ospreys started like a train, winning their first seven league games. They also won their last six, with a less consistent spell in between'

Sometimes the darkest hour is the one just before dawn. On the face of it, the 2014-15 season was as disappointing for the Welsh teams as recent ones have been. No finalist in the Guinness PRO12; no region through to the knockout stages of the European Cup. But there are definite signs of progress, and to huge relief across the land the off-the-field issues between the Welsh Rugby Union and the regions appear to have been resolved.

At the start of last season, Gareth Davies, the former national captain and Lions fly half, was contemplating his second year at the helm of Newport Gwent Dragons. A year on, and he is chairman of the union. Peace has broken out. A new financial arrangement between union and regions has been agreed, considerable progress was made with central (dual) contracts for leading members of the Welsh team, and the chief executive, Roger Lewis – focus of much discontent from those running the regional sides – announced he would stand down after the World Cup.

Once again, the Ospreys proved to be the most successful outfit. They started like a train, winning their first seven league games. They also won their last six, with a less consistent spell in between. The increasingly impressive Steve Tandy, in his second year as head coach, relied heavily on his dynamic and forceful captain Alun Wyn Jones and the half-back unit of Dan Biggar and Rhys Webb, whose top-notch form saw them established beyond any dispute as the Welsh team's halves. The on-field leadership of these three enabled a host of promising young players to develop rapidly, making their squad a force to be reckoned with.

That depth is important as key league matches are played during the Autumn International 'window' and the Six Nations. November losses in Belfast (25-16) and Dublin (18-12) together with February defeats at home to Edinburgh (24-16) and Glasgow (19-16) undermined an otherwise strong campaign which took them to third in the table, missing a home semi-final in the PRO12 play-offs by a single point. At Thomond Park they all but beat Munster in a thrilling game. What seemed to be a winning try on the final whistle was ruled out after the TMO spotted a knock-on which had gone unobserved in real time, leaving the Irish province 21-18 winners and with a place in the final.

Only a single win was recorded during their first campaign in the reworked European championship, against Benetton Treviso (42-7). In an illustration of their possibilities at this level, the Ospreys drew 19-19 at home and lost narrowly 18-14 in Le Mans to Racing, the French Top 14 quarter-finalists. Next year's grouping with Clermont, Bordeaux and Exeter could be to their liking. Paul James comes back from Bath and former Melbourne Rebels skipper Gareth Delve makes an overdue return to Wales. Their hard-earned experience will complement

FACING PAGE Ospreys captain and lock forward Alun Wyn Jones looks to offload in the tackle against Cardiff Blues.

BELOW Wing Tom Grabham beats the Blues' defence to score in the Ospreys' 31-23 Judgement Day PRO12 victory at the Millennium Stadium.

up-and-comers like loose-head Nicky Smith, lock Rory Thornton, wing Tom Grabham and fly half Sam Davies.

Scarlets finished sixth, thus guaranteeing qualification once again for the main European tournament. They were contenders for a PRO12 play-off place, winning their last four league games, but earlier results left them too much to do. A heavy defeat to Leinster (42-12) at the RDS in September did not bode well, while a 19-9 win at home to eventual champions Glasgow in November was more like it; but falling to Edinburgh at Llanelli in March (26-15) demonstrated why they could not make a top-four finish.

New Zealander Wayne Pivac was a popular and effective appointment in his first season as head coach. He oversaw encouraging home wins in European competition over Leicester Tigers (15-3) and Ulster (22-13). Next term's draw is a tough one, with Glasgow, Northampton and Racing 92 in the same pool. Personnel changes saw long-serving Mark Jones leave to become head coach at Rotherham, and valuable South African tight forwards Jacobie Adriaanse and Joe Snyman head for France, plus of course Rhys Priestland try his luck at Bath.

John Barclay, recalled to the Scotland squad, Scott and Liam Williams all had cracking seasons, as did Rob Evans, who became the newest Welshman in the national loose-head berth. DTH van de Merwe joins from Glasgow, and a full injury-free season from skipper and outstanding hooker Ken Owens would be welcome.

Despite playing well, the Dragons had a horrible start to the season in terms of results, a 33-15 win over Treviso being their only success in their first nine outings. An early home defeat (33-13) to Glasgow was an unhappy portent of things to come. Injuries again handicapped their still underpowered squad, although there were bright spots – a Boxing Day victory ten miles away at the Arms Park (23-17) was most welcome, as was doing an unlikely double over Leinster, and recording a solid 26-22 success against Ulster at Rodney Parade in March. Winning five of their last eight league games took the Dragons to ninth in the table, seven points clear of their old rivals in Cardiff.

Lyn Jones will have been disappointed at Taulupe Faletau declining a central contract but will be delighted at the progress of exciting young threequarters Hallam Amos, Tyler Morgan and Jack Dixon, who all attracted Warren Gatland's attention. A sterling shift was put in by South African Rynard Landman, the second-row and captain, who provided just the sort of leadership the eastern region required. Retirements included veterans Lee Byrne and Ian Gough, and sadly Ashley Smith – at 28 – due to concussion-related difficulties.

The Blues again had a season to forget. The appointment of former Wellington Hurricanes coach Mark Hammett as director of rugby did not work out, and before the season's end Paul John and Dale McIntosh found themselves once again in temporary charge. The latter has vacated his role of defence coach, as matters are restructured under the new and highly rated head coach Danny Wilson, previously at the Scarlets and most recently with Bristol. Graham Steadman, previously with Ireland and Scotland, takes the defence role.

On the park, Gareth Anscombe was a welcome addition, and with local talent to build upon such as Scott Andrews, Lou Reed and Josh Navidi up front and Rhys Patchell behind, the proud and famous Cardiff name must surely start the climb back towards its former prominence. It needs to. Only three wins in the PRO12 by Christmas – two against Italian teams – goes some way to explaining their lowly predicament.

London Welsh may be an exciting addition to the PRO12. With the ongoing participation of the two Italian sides in some doubt, the exiles clubs representing the Welsh and the Scots in southwest London have been sounded out as their replacements. The move has commercial and playing attraction, not least the accessibility of away matches for supporters of the existing Welsh teams.

One of the sadder moments took place after the season's end; the death in France of Jerry Collins cast a shadow for all who played and dealt with him at the Ospreys. Yet one of the happier events also took place in the close season, the knighting of the great man of Gwaun-Cae-Gurwen – arise Sir Gareth!

Ireland: Dublin Still Dominant

by RUAIDHRI O'CONNOR

'Coached by former Wales Grand Slam supremo Mike Ruddock, who guided the club to their first league win two seasons ago, Lansdowne lost just four regular season games'

ABOVE Man of the match Joe McSwiney scores his side's second try as Lansdowne come back to win the Division 1A final.

FACING PAGE Clontarf's Matthew D'Arcy, Division 1A Player of the Year, in action against Cork Con in the final of the Bateman Cup.

The era of Dublin's dominance over the Ulster Bank League Division 1A title stretched into its fifth season as Lansdowne reclaimed the trophy. Once effectively the sole property of Munster clubs and the odd interloper from Ulster, domestic honours have passed into the ownership of the eastern province in recent seasons.

Before 2010-11, St Mary's College's 2000 success had been the only win by a Leinster club since the league began in 1991, but this decade has seen Old Belvedere (2010-11), St Mary's (2011-12), Clontarf (2013-14) and Lansdowne (2012-13 and 2014-15) claim the title over five consecutive seasons.

They earned their victory through the reintroduced play-off system, seeing off Clontarf in the final on home soil at the Aviva Stadium; but by topping the table after 18 games and going into the last four as top seeds there could be no disputing who last season's premier team were.

Their supremacy hadn't been apparent all season, with newly promoted Terenure College setting the early pace on their return to the top flight. However, their challenge faltered over the winter and they ultimately fell at home to 'Tarf in the semi-finals.

That result and Lansdowne's narrow win over Young Munster in the other last-four game meant the campaign all came down to a one-point game at the national stadium, with former Munster back Scott Deasy the hero as his penalty separated the sides as Lansdowne came from behind to claim the league.

Coached by former Wales Grand Slam supremo Mike Ruddock, who guided the club to their first league win two seasons ago, Lansdowne lost just four regular season games before overcoming Young Munster in the semi-finals.

Although just two years separated the club's triumphs, Lansdowne had a significant turnover in between their league title wins and that was one of the things that satisfied Ruddock the most after they had overcome the reigning champions.

'It's very pleasing, obviously Clontarf have lost players too but the mainstay of their squad was there and they had some experienced players through the team, so it was good for us,' he said.

'We have a lot of [provincial] academy boys whom we often don't see until Thursday night. We tried to pull it together and particularly this week with exams, I planned a training day for Monday with double sessions, but half the boys had exams so we had to abandon that. Some boys couldn't make Tuesday night because of exams so we pulled it together Wednesday and Thursday, but we didn't panic because we knew we had the work we had done all season behind us.'

Perhaps the most exciting prospect to emerge for the league winners was their full back Cian Kelleher, who made his Leinster debut in the weeks after the final, while he came off the bench for Ireland against the Barbarians at the end of the campaign.

The exciting former Ireland Under 20 international was one of a host of prospects to enhance his professional credentials through league performances in a tournament with high standards as a proving ground for the big leagues.

The return of the play-off system after an absence of three seasons was broadly welcomed by those within the club game, offering players a shop window for a level of rugby that struggles for exposure despite the sport's huge growth in popularity in recent years. It created a dramatic race for the last four, with just five points separating Young Munster in fourth and St Mary's who would be relegated following a play-off.

The semi-finals and final were high-quality affairs which helped boost the league's flagging profile, even though television demands meant that the showpiece was moved to a lunchtime kick-off on the same day that Ulster faced Munster in the Guinness PRO12, which took away somewhat from the prestige.

Not that Lansdowne or Clontarf let it affect them; they played out a thrilling encounter. Clontarf led after the division's Player of the Year Matt D'Arcy – who secured a contract with Munster as a result of his endeavours – crossed for a try, but Lansdowne stormed back and Joe McSwiney touched down after his pack had mauled over, allowing Deasy to secure the 18-17 win with the boot.

Afterwards, Lansdowne's promising hooker Tyrone Moran hailed Ruddock's efforts.

'The way he coaches is fantastic; he puts a system in place and lets us step into it. We do what he wants us to do, but we just take so much pride in playing with the club,' he said.

'We're working during the day; we come down and train three nights a week usually. We train more like professionals and we've come real close together as a result.

'It's interesting because we have so many young guys in the group who want to put in performances, so somebody has to lead them, but we've also got guys like [captain] Ron Boucher and Joe McSwiney who are doing a very good job of that.'

Cork Constitution retained their stranglehold on the All Ireland Bateman Cup, claiming the trophy with a 24-9 win over Clontarf on home soil at Temple Hill. It was the Munster Senior Cup winners' third Bateman Cup triumph in successive seasons and a fitting send-off for coach Tom Tierney, who became Ireland Women's supremo midway through the season. They won away to Connacht champions Buccaneers in the semi-finals, while Clontarf overcame Ballynahinch narrowly to book their spot in the final.

There was a big boost for Connacht rugby, with Galwegians' promotion ensuring that Division 1A will have a full geographical spread for the first time since being reduced in size. Coached by Matt Brown and the province's captain John Muldoon, the westerners topped the Division 1B table, seeing off traditional powerhouses Garryowen for the automatic promotion spot by just two points at the end of a long campaign.

Indeed, it came down to the final day as the three-time champions from Limerick visited Glenina in a winner-takes-all finale which 'Wegians edged 17-13 to spark wild celebrations among the largely home-grown side whose rise further illustrated the strengthening of Connacht rugby.

'That is my proudest thing. I think there are six or seven of us alone from the junior team that won in 2008 who are now playing senior rugby at this club. That doesn't really happen to be honest or it hasn't happened very much in previous years,' captain Ja Naughton explained.

'Most of us played Under 20s together. Just take the front row there – myself, "Fitzy" [Ross Fitzgerald] and Doran McHugh all played 20s together, and then from the junior team you have Brian McClearn, Barry Lee and Brian Murphy and you had a couple of lads on the fringes of that squad as well. So, we have been playing together since we were 18s and 20s.

'We have lost players through the recession over the years – some players have had to go abroad – but anyone at home in Galway can see the standard we have at this club.'

Garryowen responded by bouncing back to defeat two-time champions St Mary's in the promotion/relegation play-off, helping to lessen the Leinster dominance in the top flight in the process. That ended the renowned Limerick club's one-year stay in the second tier, but Ireland's most successful club, Shannon, remain outside the top tier after enduring a middling season in Division 1B. Former Munster and Ireland loose-head Marcus Horan has been charged with resurrecting Shannon's fortunes next season as the nine-time champions continue to languish outside of the elite.

Another fallen giant, Blackrock College, will be back in Division 1B next season after securing automatic promotion from Division 2A along with champions Old Wesley, with Ulster's Malone and Connacht's Corinthians dropping into the third tier.

That division and Division 2B are both being restructured next season, with a fifth tier being created so that each division consists of ten teams in 2015-16, which means Division 2B winners Highfield are one of four clubs to join Division 2A from the old 2B.

The latest addition to the senior club ranks will be Dundalk RFC after the Louth side came out on top of the qualification round robin; they will replace Ulster's Ards in Division 2C next season.

Overall, it was an excellent season in terms of quality in the All Ireland League, but it continues to struggle to find a place amid the demands of the professional game. The value of it as a proving ground will be seen during the World Cup, when the provinces rely heavily on club players to get through without their internationals, while a host of players like Darragh Fanning, Craig Ronaldson and Matt Healy have shown how to use it as a stepping stone into the big leagues.

The streamlining of the league should help improve the product, and the challenge for those outside the capital is to break the Dublin clubs' stranglehold on the competition next season. With half of the participants hailing from Leinster, it won't be an easy task.

France: Novès Gets the Nod

by CHRIS THAU

'Novès started his senior playing career with Toulouse 40 years ago. He played 259 matches for the club, mostly on the wing, and coached the club in 749 matches'

Several weeks before France's head coach Philippe Saint-André announced his country's 36-strong squad for RWC 2015, the French Federation, with an 'immaculate' sense of timing, released the name of his successor! The only rationale behind this rather unseemly rush must be political, as politics do often dictate the course of events in the corridors of power of Marcoussis, the headquarters of French rugby. The seven-man commission chaired by FFR president Pierre Camou had shortlisted eight of the 66 candidates who applied for the job, a shortlist which included Toulouse coach Guy Novès, former England coach Sir Clive Woodward and two former French captains, Fabien Galthié and Raphaël Ibanez, both high-profile and successful coaches.

Somewhat expectedly, the commission elected the 61-year-old Novès, arguably the most successful club coach in French and probably international rugby, as the new coach of France. Unlike in 2011, when he turned down the offer to take over from Marc Lièvremont in the aftermath of the Rugby World Cup, Novès accepted this time and will replace Saint-André at the beginning of November. Reports in French media suggest that Novès' decision to apply for the France job may have had to do with an increasingly tense relationship with the Stade Toulousain president, René Bouscatel, as well as a series of unrelated conflicts involving high-profile members of the management committee. The comparative failure, by Toulouse standards, to secure any silverware this season must have complicated the matter further, especially since Novès' men got knocked out in the semi-finals of the Top 14 against eternal rivals Clermont Auvergne. The feeling among those close to the top of the complex Toulouse club structure was that the time had arrived for a change, and Novès, who had run the club with an iron hand for the past 20-odd years, must have been made aware of the prevailing sentiment.

Novès started his senior playing career with Toulouse 40 years ago and stepped down in June this year, after 23 consecutive seasons as club coach and manager. He played 259 matches for the club, mostly on the wing, and coached the club in 749 matches. He made his international debut on 11 November 1977 in a famous French win against the visiting All Blacks in a team captained by Jacques Fouroux, and retired from international rugby seven caps and two years later criticizing the French establishment for lack of care and respect. He may have had a point. However, he carried on with his club rugby career and played for the celebrated Red and Black team of 1985, who won the championship that year and the year after, to end 38 years of silverware famine.

With Novès at the helm, Toulouse established itself as the leading club in Europe, winning 18 trophies – ten French Championship titles, four Heineken Cups, one Yves du Manoir Challenge, one French Cup, one Champions' Trophy and one de Coubertin Trophy. He will be missed by many, especially among the players, who have a huge regard for the man. 'When I think of him, I think of the thirst for winning. His whole life seems closely related to the desire to overcome and to constantly improve,' former Toulouse and France captain Fabien Pelous said. 'Guy Novès first talks to the man, before he addresses the player. Simply I love Guy Novès and his approach,' observed Toulouse hooker Corey Flynn. 'He helped me grow up both as a player and as a man,' said Maxime Médard. 'He knows how to read people like a book. His ability to identify characters to make the most of the individual has no equivalent. All players who have gone through the Stade have respect for this man,' Pelous added.

It has been announced already that one of Novès' former Toulouse players and apprentices Ugo Mola, an international full back and utility player, will take over as Toulouse head coach, while Novès has recruited as his assistants for the national team two other former Toulouse players: his former forwards coach Yannick Bru, who is one of Saint-André's coaching team, and the youthful Jean-Frédéric 'Jeff' Dubois, the backs coach of Stade Français. The spirit of Toulouse shines bright!

Unperturbed by the fuss, Saint-André has commenced working alongside his faithful partners – forwards coach Bru and Patrice Lagisquet, the backs coach – on the final touches of what might well be a conclusive climax of a capricious international coaching career. 'This is the beginning of a wonderful adventure, something we have been awaiting for three years,' he said, meaning in fact, 'Don't judge me on what has gone on so far, wait until the end of the RWC.' He may still surprise a few, a view shared by one of his devotees, Kingsley Jones, a former assistant coach at Sale and head coach of Russia, currently coaching Newport Gwent Dragons.

So far, a combination of factors, of which time is probably the most significant, has prevented the perfectionist coach from attaining the quality of output he and his fellow coaches have been looking for. The time factor, at least, has now been addressed in the form of 75 days of squad preparation, an absolute godsend for what Saint-André and his coaching team preach and practise. There have been glimpses of what France could do in their defeat by England in the final Six Nations game. Eliminate the unforced errors and expand that ebullient, creative frame of mind to 80 minutes and who knows, 'Le Goret' might have the last laugh after all.

Unfortunately, due to the poor co-ordination between the federation and the professional league, Saint-André is limited to a squad of no more than 36 players in the build-up to the RWC. This is why the talented Jules Plisson, who is nursing an injury and most certainly would have been in the enlarged squad, and Antoine Burban, the fiery Stade Français flanker who had a sensational end of season, making a significant contribution to Stade's success in the Top 14 final, are not at Marcoussis, though things may hopefully change. The success of the French Sevens team, who topped the European rankings to qualify for the Rio Olympics, might just inspire the senior side to higher honours this autumn.

The final stages of the exciting French Championship brought to the fore Stade Français, a team dismissed by most pundits as a collection of 'nobodies', 'has-beens' and 'maybes' compared to the

start-studded list of their opponents in the knockout stages: Racing Métro 92, Toulon, and Clermont in the final. The team, coached by Argentine kicking prodigy Gonzalo Quesada and captained by the charismatic Italian skipper Sergio Parisse, answered the headline 'Stade who?' in emphatic manner. 'We became aware of our potential after the quarter-final when we managed to defeat Racing [38-15], though we played with 14 men for nearly an hour. That was the day we reached the final, not the day when we beat Toulon,' observed Antoine Burban, whose energy and overall contribution managed to impress the French selectors.

The final itself was an anticlimax, finals always are, with Stade Français' Morné Steyn, who landed four penalties, winning the kicking duel with the Clermont trio of Morgan Parra, Brock James and Camille Lopez, who managed two successful kicks between them, for a final scoreline of 12-6. And if the result of the final, a repeat of the 2007 Top 14 decider, was remarkable in itself, bringing the Parisian club its fourteenth championship title since 1893, the demolition of star-studded Toulon in the semi-final was positively astonishing. It was an extraordinary sight to see the Toulon scrummage slowly crushed by the Stade forwards, who were coached by another unknown, Adrien Buononato. Had anybody heard of him before this match?

The Toulon front row were made to suffer by Heinke van der Merwe, Rémi Bonfils (and his replacement Laurent Sempéré) and Rabah Slimani. Captain Parisse was in imperious form, supported by two ferociously efficient flankers in Burban and Raphaël Lakafia. The Toulon ambush was carefully planned by the 41-year-old Quesada and his team of forwards coach Buononato, backs coach Jeff Dubois and fitness and conditioning coach Alex Marco, all completely unknown until the recent championship finals. Quesada himself was more famous for his kicking exploits in RWC 1999 than for any coaching feat, especially since one has to admit that the kicking feats of the French in the final of RWC 2011, when he was employed as France's kicking coach, did not do much to enhance his status. The technical aspects of what has been achieved by Quesada and co. will still be analysed by experts in the months to come. What cannot be identified by video-analysts, however, is the youthful euphoria within the Stade Français ranks that enabled Parisse and his players to rediscover the values of playing for pleasure and your mates.

Italy: Gavazzi's Double Whammy

by CHRIS THAU

'The same intolerable level of unforced errors that seemed to beset every facet of the Italian game plagued the Eccellenza final, a repeat of last year's in everything but score'

There is no love lost between the Italian players and the president of the federation, Alfredo Gavazzi. While the substance of Gavazzi's end-of-season tirade in the aftermath of the Six Nations campaign, chastising the Italian team as 'pensioners', was inappropriate, the timing of his attempt to restructure the financial deal between the federation and the international squad just before the Rugby World Cup was even more unfortunate. Rightly or wrongly Gavazzi felt that the bonus scheme operating so far should be replaced by an incentive package, comparable, as he put it, to the arrangements functioning elsewhere in unions of Italy's standard and ranking.

ABOVE FIR president Alfredo Gavazzi (left) with national head coach Jacques Brunel in 2013. Gavazzi caused a storm this year with his remarks about the Italian team and his efforts to restructure the international players' financial package.

Had he tried to review the financial arrangements without calling Italian players names, he may have succeeded, though this is by no means certain. But his astonishingly ill-judged comments managed to unite and antagonize the players like never before. Following the reaction of Italy's captain and talisman Sergio Parisse on Twitter, a wave of messages in the social media from the Italian players demanded 'respect'. Instead of trying to play down the unfortunate incident just before the Italian RWC squad was to gather for its first camp in Villabassa, Gavazzi announced his incentive scheme, apparently without discussing it with the Italian players' association. Call this a red cape waved in front of a raging bull!

Unsurprisingly the players selected for the initial three-week RWC camp refused to train or wear the appropriate kit, until a satisfactory agreement was negotiated. To Jacques Brunel's relief, sanity prevailed in the end and the Italian Federation and the players' representatives reached a mutually satisfactory agreement, but the resentment is still there. Parisse – also the captain of the new French champion club Stade Français, who delayed his arrival in Villabassa in order to play in the French Top 14 final – did not mince his words. 'The final was the happiest day of my life as an athlete. But I was disappointed not to have received a phone call from the President of our Federation. I thought he should have felt honoured to have the captain of his national team on the pitch with the Italian flag and the Bouclier de Brennus,' he said.

Unfortunately Parisse, born in Argentina 32 years ago, is approaching the end of his glorious career, so it will be Gavazzi who is likely to have the last word in this dispute. However, rather than pick fights with his international players the FIR president should concentrate on elite development, the source of all evils in Italian rugby. Although the Italian Under 20s managed an escape act against Samoa in their final match of the World Rugby U20 Championship, the news is not that good. Two penalty tries secured Alessandro Troncon's

BELOW Italy Under 20 celebrate beating Samoa Under 20 by the skin of their teeth to remain in the Championship competition for next year. Italy have led a somewhat yo-yo existence in Under 20 rugby, having gone up and down between the Trophy and Championship tournaments.

FACING PAGE Tommaso Castello, with Alberto Bergamo in support, takes on the Rovigo defence as Calvisano win the Eccellenza final 11-10.

team a hard-fought 20-19 win, but very few of them showed that they could be ready for the next step up the ladder.

The same intolerable level of unforced errors that seemed to beset every facet of the Italian game plagued the Eccellenza (Italian League) final, a repeat of last year's in everything but score. Cammi Calvisano defeated Femi-CZ Rovigo 11-10 in an eminently forgettable game, spoiled by the sending-off of Calvisano prop Salvatore Costanzo for stamping after some 25 minutes of play. Each team scored a try – for Calvisano it was right wing Gabriele Di Giulio, while for Rovigo it was skipper Luke Mahoney, who came on to replace wing Francesco Menon. New Zealand-born outside half Ben Seymour landed two penalties for Calvisano, while South African full back Stefan Basson kicked a penalty and a conversion for Rovigo. 'When you lose a game after playing for nearly an hour against fourteen men you have to congratulate your opponent. Calvisano today deserved to win more than we did,' Rovigo captain Luke Mahoney said.

Calvisano's less heralded yet nevertheless highly beneficial by-product of the season was their success in the European Rugby Challenge Cup qualifying competition, organized by EPCR in conjunction with Rugby Europe and the Italian Federation and probably Europe's best-kept rugby secret. In addition to three Italian clubs, the innovative qualifying concept involved clubs from four other Continental countries: Spain, Portugal, Russia and Romania. The Georgian Union declined to take part this season, but they will eventually join, probably after the Rugby World Cup. At the end of the qualifying process, two of the eight competing clubs – Cammi Calvisano of Italy and Enisei STM of Russia – have booked their places in the 2015-16 European Rugby Challenge Cup, having knocked out Rovigo and Romanian champions Baia Mare respectively in the play-offs. This is the first time a Russian club will have played in the 20-strong Challenge Cup competition.

A Summary of the Season 2014-15

by TERRY COOPER

INTERNATIONAL RUGBY

AUSTRALIA TO EUROPE, NOVEMBER 2014

Opponents	Results
Barbarians	W 40-36
WALES	W 33-28
FRANCE	L 26-29
IRELAND	L 23-26
ENGLAND	L 17-26

Played 5 Won 2 Lost 3

NEW ZEALAND TO USA & UK, NOVEMBER 2014

Opponents	Results
USA	W 74-6
ENGLAND	W 24-21
SCOTLAND	W 24-16
WALES	W 34-16

Played 4 Won 4

SOUTH AFRICA TO EUROPE, NOVEMBER 2014

Opponents	Results
IRELAND	L 15-29
ENGLAND	W 31-28
ITALY	W 22-6
WALES	L 6-12

Played 4 Won 2 Lost 2

ARGENTINA TO EUROPE, NOVEMBER 2014

Opponents	Results
SCOTLAND	L 31-41
ITALY	W 20-18
FRANCE	W 18-13

Played 3 Won 2 Lost 1

CANADA TO EUROPE, NOVEMBER 2014

Opponents	Results
RFU Championship XV	L 23-28
NAMIBIA (at Colwyn Bay)	W 17-13
SAMOA (at Vannes, France)	L 13-23
ROMANIA	L 9-18

Played 4 Won 1 Lost 3

TONGA TO EUROPE, NOVEMBER 2014

Opponents	Results
GEORGIA	W 23-9
USA (at Gloucester)	W 40-12
SCOTLAND	L 12-37

Played 3 Won 2 Lost 1

FIJI TO EUROPE, NOVEMBER 2014

Opponents	Results
FRANCE	L 15-40
WALES	L 13-17
USA (at Vannes, France)	W 20-14

Played 3 Won 1 Lost 2

SAMOA TO EUROPE, NOVEMBER 2014

Opponents	Results
ITALY	L 13-24
CANADA (at Vannes, France)	W 23-13
ENGLAND	L 9-28

Played 3 Won 1 Lost 2

OTHER INTERNATIONAL MATCHES 2014

Australia	28	New Zealand	29
(Bledisloe Cup; see also The Rugby Championship)			
Ireland	49	Georgia	7

ROYAL BANK OF SCOTLAND
6 NATIONS CHAMPIONSHIP 2015

Results

Wales	16	England	21
Italy	3	Ireland	26
France	15	Scotland	8
England	47	Italy	17
Ireland	18	France	11
Scotland	23	Wales	26
Scotland	19	Italy	22
France	13	Wales	20
Ireland	19	England	9
Wales	23	Ireland	16
England	25	Scotland	13
Italy	0	France	29
Italy	20	Wales	61
Scotland	10	Ireland	40
England	55	France	35

Final Table

	P	W	D	L	F	A	PD	Pts
Ireland	5	4	0	1	119	56	63	8
England	5	4	0	1	157	100	57	8
Wales	5	4	0	1	146	93	53	8
France	5	2	0	3	103	101	2	4
Italy	5	1	0	4	62	182	-120	2
Scotland	5	0	0	5	73	128	-55	0

WOMEN'S SIX NATIONS 2015

Results

Italy	5	Ireland	30
France	42	Scotland	0
Wales	13	England	0
Ireland	5	France	10
Scotland	3	Wales	39
England	39	Italy	7
Ireland	11	England	8
France	28	Wales	7
Scotland	8	Italy	31
England	42	Scotland	13
Italy	17	France	12
Wales	0	Ireland	20
Italy	22	Wales	5
England	15	France	21
Scotland	3	Ireland	73

Final Table

	P	W	D	L	F	A	PD	Pts
Ireland	5	4	0	1	139	26	113	8
France	5	4	0	1	113	44	69	8
Italy	5	3	0	2	82	94	-12	6
England	5	2	0	3	104	65	39	4
Wales	5	2	0	3	64	73	-9	4
Scotland	5	0	0	5	27	227	-200	0

UNDER 20 SIX NATIONS 2015

Results

Italy	15	Ireland	47
Wales	21	England	15
France	47	Scotland	6
Scotland	36	Wales	34
Ireland	37	France	20
England	61	Italy	0

Ireland	14	England	19
Scotland	45	Italy	0
France	27	Wales	5
England	26	Scotland	11
Italy	10	France	40
Wales	19	Ireland	12
Italy	21	Wales	23
Scotland	17	Ireland	10
England	24	France	11

Final Table

	P	W	D	L	F	A	PD	Pts
England	5	4	0	1	145	57	88	8
France	5	3	0	2	145	82	63	6
Scotland	5	3	0	2	115	117	-2	6
Wales	5	3	0	2	102	111	-9	6
Ireland	5	2	0	3	120	90	30	4
Italy	5	0	0	5	46	216	-170	0

WORLD RUGBY
PACIFIC NATIONS CUP 2015

(Held in July and August)

Fiji	30	Tonga	22
Canada	6	Japan	20
USA	16	Samoa	21
Fiji	30	Samoa	30
Canada	18	Tonga	28
USA	23	Japan	18
USA	19	Tonga	33
Fiji	27	Japan	22
Canada	20	Samoa	21

Fifth-place Play-off

USA	15	Canada	13

Third-place Play-off

Tonga	31	Japan	20

Final

Fiji	39	Samoa	29

WORLD RUGBY NATIONS CUP 2015

(Held in June in Bucharest, Romania)

Namibia	10	Argentina Jaguars	30
Romania	35	Spain	9
Argentina Jaguars	15	Spain	6
Romania	43	Namibia	3
Spain	20	Namibia	3
Romania	23	Argentina Jaguars	0

Champions: Romania
Runners-up: Argentina Jaguars

EUROPEAN NATIONS CUP 2014-16
DIVISION 1A – FIRST LEG (2015)

Final Table

	P	W	D	L	F	A	BP	Pts
Georgia	5	5	0	0	158	42	1	21
Romania	5	3	0	2	102	61	3	15
Spain	5	3	0	2	131	99	2	14
Russia	5	3	0	2	103	119	1	13
Portugal	5	1	0	4	52	100	1	5
Germany	5	0	0	5	61	186	1	1

Your retirement *nest egg* could become a source of income PROFITS.

NOW THAT the pension rules are changing, there are more ways to feather your retirement nest. With income funds, for example. And no-one knows more about income territory than the Artemis hunters. We have expert Profit hunters in Strategic Bonds, Income, Global Income and Monthly Distribution. Each offering a compelling alternative to putting all of your nest egg into one annuity basket. Please remember that past performance should not be seen as a guide to future performance. The value of an investment and any income from it can fall as well as rise as a result of market and currency fluctuations and you may not get back the amount originally invested.

Fig. 1:
A typical PROFIT

ARTEMIS
The PROFIT Hunter

0800 092 2051   *investorsupport@artemisfunds.com*   *artemis.co.uk*

Issued by Artemis Fund Managers Limited which is authorised and regulated by the Financial Conduct Authority (www.fca.org.uk), 25 The North Colonnade, Canary Wharf, London E14 5HS. For your protection calls are usually recorded. The Portfolio Adviser Fund Awards 2015 Readers' Choice Award was awarded to Artemis Investment Management LLP. Portfolio Adviser is circulated to investment advisers, discretionary managers, wealth managers, private client stockbrokers, trustees and fund selectors.

WORLD RUGBY U20 CHAMPIONSHIP 2015

(Held in June in Italy)

Semi-finals

New Zealand	45	France	7
South Africa	20	England	28

Third-place Play-off

France	18	South Africa	31

Final

New Zealand	21	England	16

WORLD RUGBY U20 TROPHY 2015

(Held in May in Lisbon, Portugal)

Seventh-place Play-off

Portugal	47	Hong Kong	21

Fifth-place Play-off

Fiji	36	Namibia	24

Third-place Play-off

Uruguay	44	Tonga	43

Final

Georgia	49	Canada	24

RUGBY EUROPE U18 CHAMPIONSHIP 2015 – ELITE DIVISION

(Held in March/April in France)

Semi-finals

England	19	France	23
Georgia	6	Italy	6

(Georgia won 5-4 on penalties)

Third-place Play-off

England	39	Italy	12

Final

France	57	Georgia	0

THE RUGBY CHAMPIONSHIP 2014

Results

*Australia	12	New Zealand	12
South Africa	13	Argentina	6
*New Zealand	51	Australia	20
Argentina	31	South Africa	33
New Zealand	28	Argentina	9
Australia	24	South Africa	23
New Zealand	14	South Africa	10
Australia	32	Argentina	25
South Africa	28	Australia	10
Argentina	13	New Zealand	34
South Africa	27	New Zealand	25
Argentina	21	Australia	17

*These fixtures were simultaneously Rugby Championship and Bledisloe Cup matches; New Zealand were the cup winners; see also page 144.

Final Table

	P	W	D	L	PD	BP	Pts
New Zealand	6	4	1	1	73	4	22
South Africa	6	4	0	2	24	3	19
Australia	6	2	1	3	-45	1	11
Argentina	6	1	0	5	-52	3	7

HSBC SEVENS WORLD SERIES FINALS 2014-15

Australia (Gold Coast)

Fiji	31	Samoa	24

Dubai

Australia	7	South Africa	33

South Africa (Port Elizabeth)

South Africa	26	New Zealand	17

New Zealand (Wellington)

England	21	New Zealand	27

USA (Las Vegas)

Fiji	35	New Zealand	19

Hong Kong

Fiji	33	New Zealand	19

Japan (Tokyo)

South Africa	14	England	21

Scotland (Glasgow)

Fiji	24	New Zealand	17

England (Twickenham)

Australia	22	USA	45

Champions: Fiji

Note: The first four teams qualify automatically for the 2016 Olympic Games in Rio de Janeiro. In qualifying order they are: Fiji, South Africa, New Zealand and England.

WORLD RUGBY WOMEN'S SEVENS SERIES FINALS 2014-15

Dubai

Australia	17	New Zealand	19

Brazil (São Paulo)

New Zealand	17	Australia	10

USA (Atlanta)

New Zealand	50	USA	12

Canada (Langford)

Russia	10	New Zealand	29

England (Twickenham Stoop)

Canada	17	Australia	20

Netherlands (Amsterdam)

Australia	17	Canada	20

Champions: New Zealand

Note: The first four teams qualify automatically for the 2016 Olympic Games in Rio de Janeiro. In qualifying order they are: New Zealand, Canada, Australia and England.

CLUB, COUNTY AND DIVISIONAL RUGBY

ENGLAND

Aviva Premiership

	P	W	D	L	F	A	BP	Pts
Northampton	22	16	1	5	621	400	10	76
Bath	22	16	0	6	625	414	11	75
Leicester	22	15	1	6	453	421	6	68
Saracens	22	14	1	7	664	418	10	68
Exeter	22	14	0	8	663	437	12	68
Wasps	22	11	2	9	672	527	13	61
Sale	22	11	0	11	497	482	10	54
Harlequins	22	10	0	12	444	514	9	49
Gloucester	22	9	1	12	553	575	10	46
London Irish	22	7	1	14	442	578	10	40
Newcastle	22	5	1	16	475	545	12	34
London Welsh	22	0	0	22	223	1021	1	1

Relegated: London Welsh

Aviva Premiership Play-offs
Semi-finals
Northampton	24	Saracens	29
Bath	47	Leicester	10

Final
Bath	16	Saracens	28

Greene King IPA Championship Play-offs
Semi-finals (1st leg)
Bristol	32	Rotherham Titans	20
London Scottish	22	Worcester	27

Semi-finals (2nd leg)
Worcester	38	London Scottish	15
Rotherham Titans	16	Bristol	24

Final
Bristol	28	Worcester	29
Worcester	30	Bristol	30

Promoted to Premiership: Worcester

National Leagues
National 1 Champions: Ealing Trailfinders
Runners-up: Rosslyn Park
National 2 (S) Champions: Henley
Runners-up: Bishop's Stortford
National 2 (N) Champions: Hull Ionians
Runners-up: Ampthill

National 2 N & S Runners-up Play-off
Ampthill	19	Bishop's Stortford	10

RFU Knockout Trophies Finals
Intermediate Cup
Maidstone	31	Bridgnorth	18

Senior Vase
West Leeds	10	Bromley	16

Junior Vase
Battersea Ironsides	30	Longlevens	15

County Championships
Bill Beaumont Cup Division 1 Final
Lancashire	13	Cornwall	18

Bill Beaumont Cup Division 2 (Plate) Final
Eastern Counties	3	Surrey	17

County Championship Shield Final
Leicestershire	34	Cumbria	17

National U20 Championship Final
Yorkshire	36	Berkshire	3

National Under 17 Cup Final
Nottingham Corsairs	21	Sevenoaks	20

Oxbridge University Matches
Varsity Match
Oxford	43	Cambridge	6

Under 21 Varsity Match
Oxford	36	Cambridge	12

Women's Varsity Match
Oxford	0	Cambridge	47

BUCS Competitions
Men's Championship Winners: Leeds Beckett
Women's Championship Winners: Gloucestershire

Inter-Service Championship
Royal Navy	32	Royal Air Force	32
Royal Air Force	33	Army	29
Army	36	Royal Navy	18

Champions: RAF

Hospitals Cup Winners: RUMS RFC

Rosslyn Park Schools Sevens
Open Winners: Wellington College
Festival Winners: Stowe School
Colts Winners: Reigate Grammar School
Preparatory Winners: Caldicott
Juniors Winners: Dulwich College
Girls Winners: Amman Valley School
Girls AASE Winners: Hartpury College A

NatWest Schools Cup Finals Day
Under 18 Cup Winners: Bromsgrove
Under 18 Vase Winners: Churcher's College
Under 15 Cup Winners: QEGS Wakefield
Under 15 Vase Winners: Sherborne

Women's Premiership

	P	W	D	L	F	A	BP	Pts
Saracens	14	12	0	2	464	130	11	59
Richmond	14	12	1	1	458	170	7	57
Worcester	14	7	1	6	326	277	6	36
Bristol	14	6	0	8	414	269	11	35
Lichfield	14	6	2	6	277	290	4	32
Wasps	14	5	0	9	240	270	8	28
DMP Sharks	14	5	0	9	216	329	3	23
Aylesford Bulls	14	1	0	13	94	754	2	6

SCOTLAND

BT Cup Final
Hawick   17   Boroughmuir   55

BT Shield Final
GHK   19   St Boswells   27

BT Bowl Final
Alloa   71   Cumnock   19

Scottish Sevens Winners
Gala: Gala
Melrose: Glasgow Warriors
Berwick: Gala
Langholm: Hawick
Peebles: Gala
Kelso: Melrose
Earlston: Melrose
Selkirk: Jed-Forest
Hawick: Hawick
Jed-Forest: Jed-Forest
Kings of the Sevens: Gala

BT Premiership

	P	W	D	L	F	A	BP	Pts
Heriot's	18	13	0	5	501	339	16	68
Ayr	18	12	0	6	392	331	10	58
Melrose	18	12	0	6	402	331	9	57
Currie	18	9	2	7	379	382	6	46
Gala	18	9	0	9	380	354	9	45
Hawick	18	8	1	9	354	414	9	43
Glasgow Hawks	18	7	1	10	310	302	7	37
Boroughmuir	18	8	0	10	306	427	5	37
Stirling County	18	5	0	13	372	411	15	35
Edinburgh Acads	18	5	0	13	279	384	8	28

BT Premiership Play-off Final
Heriot's   22   Melrose   20

BT National League Division 1

	P	W	D	L	F	A	BP	Pts
Selkirk	22	22	0	0	646	281	13	101
GHA	22	17	1	4	559	411	12	82
Stewart's Melville	22	14	2	6	577	357	17	77
Watsonians	22	13	0	9	570	381	13	65
Dundee HSFP	22	13	1	8	513	396	10	64
Peebles	22	9	2	11	461	424	11	51
Aberdeen GS	22	9	1	12	553	571	13	51
Jed-Forest	22	8	1	13	455	467	10	44
Kelso	22	7	3	12	440	470	10	44
Marr	22	7	3	12	537	593	9	43
Biggar	22	6	0	16	340	558	6	30
Hillhead J'hill	22	0	0	22	213	955	3	3

BT Premiership-National 1 Play-off
GHA   22   Stirling County   39

BT Women's Premier League
Champions: Murrayfield Wanderers

Sarah Beaney Cup
Winners: Murrayfield Wanderers

WALES

SSE SWALEC Cup Final
Pontypridd   15   Bridgend   19

SSE SWALEC Plate Final
Newcastle Emlyn   17   Ystrad Rhondda   25

SSE SWALEC Bowl Final
Cambrian Welfare   12   Ystradgynlais   17

Principality Premiership

	P	W	D	L	F	A	BP	Pts
*Pontypridd	22	21	0	1	673	253	14	94
Ebbw Vale	22	15	0	7	539	402	13	73
Cross Keys	22	15	1	6	599	449	9	71
Cardiff	22	12	0	10	483	471	12	60
Bedwas	22	11	0	11	579	535	16	60
C'marthen Quins	22	12	0	10	590	488	11	59
Aberavon	22	10	0	12	411	448	8	48
Llandovery	22	9	1	12	482	464	9	47
Llanelli	22	8	1	13	542	728	11	45
Neath	22	7	0	15	378	559	8	36
Bridgend	22	5	1	16	418	706	9	31
Newport	22	5	0	17	372	563	9	29

*Pontypridd received a deduction of four league points for the inclusion of an ineligible player.

SSE SWALEC Championship

	P	W	D	L	F	A	BP	Pts
Bargoed	26	25	0	1	958	362	24	124
Swansea	26	22	0	4	909	386	19	107
Merthyr	26	19	0	7	671	452	13	89
RGC 1404	26	15	0	11	848	436	23	83
Pontypool	26	16	0	10	639	483	13	77
Narberth	26	15	1	10	542	562	8	70
Cardiff Met	26	14	0	12	648	533	10	66
Bridgend Ath	26	14	0	12	496	465	9	65
Tata Steel	26	12	0	14	486	651	10	58
Glynneath	26	9	0	17	532	653	7	43
Newbridge	26	7	1	18	479	777	9	39
Llanharan	26	6	0	20	475	663	9	33
Tondu	26	4	0	22	461	717	14	30
Blackwood	26	3	0	23	368	1372	8	20

SSE SWALEC Leagues
Division 1 East Champions: Penallta
Division 1 North Champions: Pwllheli
Division 1 West Champions: Newcastle Emlyn

Women's Super Cup Finals
Cup Final
Skewen   31   Pontyclun Falcons   12
Plate Final
Pencoed   26   Seven Sisters   19
Bowl Final
Haverfordwest   17   Ynysybwl   10
Vase Final
Porth Harlequins   19   Wattstown   10
Under 18 Final
Cardiff Quins   54   Wattstown   3

IRELAND

Ulster Bank League Division 1A

	P	W	D	L	F	A	BP	Pts
Lansdowne	18	14	0	4	396	272	9	65
Terenure College	18	11	0	7	422	304	9	53
Clontarf	18	10	0	8	410	322	12	52
Young Munster	18	9	0	9	297	361	7	43
Old Belvedere	18	7	1	10	357	313	12	42
UCD	18	8	1	9	375	402	7	41
Ballynahinch	18	8	1	9	369	397	7	41
Cork Constitution	18	7	2	9	269	303	7	39
St Mary's College	18	8	0	10	349	409	6	38
Dolphin	18	4	3	11	255	416	5	27

Ulster Bank League Division 1A Final
Lansdowne 18 Clontarf 17

Ulster Bank League Division 1B

	P	W	D	L	F	A	BP	Pts
Galwegians	18	14	0	4	377	318	11	67
Garryowen	18	14	0	4	406	259	9	65
Dublin University	18	13	1	4	462	278	10	64
Ballymena	18	11	1	6	386	265	8	54
Belfast 'Quins	18	8	0	10	402	376	7	39
Shannon	18	7	0	11	311	378	8	36
Buccaneers	18	7	1	10	287	420	5	35
UL Bohemian	18	6	0	12	280	371	8	32
Malone	18	5	0	13	314	409	6	26
Corinthians	18	3	1	14	249	400	7	21

Ulster Bank League Division 1A Play-off
St Mary's College 3 Garryowen 13

Ulster Bank League Division 2A
Champions: Old Wesley

Ulster Bank League Division 2B
Champions: Highfield

Round Robin

Clonmel	40	Connemara	0
Instonians	11	Dundalk	15
Connemara	0	Instonians	40
Dundalk	24	Clonmel	8
Connemara	28	Dundalk	48
Instonians	27	Clonmel	37

Winners: Dundalk

All Ireland Cup Final
Cork Constitution 24 Clontarf 9

All Ireland Junior Cup Final
Bangor 5 Dundalk 55

Fraser McMullen Under 21 Cup Final
Dublin University 15 Lansdowne 16

GUINNESS PRO12 2014-15

	P	W	D	L	F	A	BP	Pts
Glasgow	22	16	1	5	540	360	9	75
Munster	22	15	2	5	581	367	11	75
Ospreys	22	16	1	5	546	358	8	74
Ulster	22	14	2	6	524	372	9	69
Leinster	22	11	3	8	483	375	12	62
Scarlets	22	11	3	8	452	388	7	57
Connacht	22	10	1	11	447	419	8	50
Edinburgh	22	10	1	11	399	419	6	48
Dragons	22	8	0	14	393	484	10	42
Blues	22	7	1	14	430	545	5	35
Treviso	22	3	1	18	306	641	5	19
Zebre	22	3	0	19	266	639	3	15

Guinness PRO12 Play-offs
Semi-finals

Glasgow	16	Ulster	14
Munster	21	Ospreys	18

Final

Munster	13	Glasgow	31

LV= CUP 2014-15

Semi-finals

Saracens	24	Northampton	20
Leicester	22	Exeter	30

Final

Saracens	23	Exeter	20

BRITISH & IRISH CUP 2014-15

Final

Doncaster Knights	5	Worcester	35

FRANCE

'Top 14' 2014-15 Play-offs

Semi-finals

Toulon	16	Stade Français	33
Clermont Auvergne	18	Toulouse	14

Final

Clermont Auvergne	6	Stade Français	12

ITALY

Campionato Italiano d'Eccellenza 2014-15

Final
Rovigo   10   Cammi Calvisano   11

EUROPEAN RUGBY CHAMPIONS CUP 2014-15

Quarter-finals
Leinster   18   Bath   15
Clermont Auvergne   37   Northampton   5
Racing Métro 92   11   Saracens   12
Toulon   32   Wasps   18

Semi-finals
Clermont Auvergne   13   Saracens   9
Toulon   25   Leinster   20

Final
Clermont Auvergne   18   Toulon   24

EUROPEAN RUGBY CHALLENGE CUP 2014-15

Quarter-finals
Gloucester   14   Connacht   7
Dragons   25   Blues   21
Exeter   48   Newcastle   13
London Irish   18   Edinburgh   23

Semi-finals
Edinburgh   45   Dragons   16
Gloucester   30   Exeter   19

Final
Edinburgh   13   Gloucester   19

NEW ZEALAND

ITM Cup Premiership Final 2014

Taranaki   36   Tasman   32

ITM Cup Championship Final 2014

Manawatu   32   Hawke's Bay   24

Heartland Champions 2014
Meads Cup: Mid Canterbury
Lochore Cup: Wanganui

Ranfurly Shield holders: Hawke's Bay

SOUTH AFRICA

Currie Cup 2014

Final
Western Province   19   Golden Lions   16

SUPER RUGBY 2015

	P	W	D	L	F	A	BP	Pts
Hurricanes	16	14	0	2	458	288	10	66
Waratahs	16	11	0	5	409	313	8	52
Stormers	16	10	1	5	373	323	3	45
Highlanders	16	11	0	5	450	333	9	53
Chiefs	16	10	0	6	372	299	8	48
Brumbies	16	9	0	7	369	261	11	47
Crusaders	16	9	0	7	481	338	10	46
Lions	16	9	1	6	342	364	4	42
Bulls	16	7	0	9	397	388	10	38
Rebels	16	7	0	9	319	354	8	36
Sharks	16	7	0	9	338	401	5	34
Cheetahs	16	5	0	11	357	531	6	26
Reds	16	4	0	12	247	434	6	22
Blues	16	3	0	13	282	428	8	20
Force	16	3	0	13	245	384	7	19

Qualifiers
Highlanders   24   Chiefs   14
Stormers   19   Brumbies   39

Semi-finals
Hurricanes   29   Brumbies   9
Waratahs   17   Highlanders   35

Final
Hurricanes   14   Highlanders   21

Key
Hurricanes: Conference leaders
Highlanders: Wild Card teams

Note: The top two Conference leaders –
Hurricanes and Waratahs – received a bye to the
semi-finals.

BARBARIANS

Opponents	Results
Australia XV	L 36-40
Leicester Tigers	W 59-26
Combined Services	W 31-15
Heriot's	W 97-31
Ireland XV	W 22-21
England XV	L 12-73

Played 6 Won 4 Lost 2

We start with the finest ingredients

RWC Breakfast now available at Loch Fyne in Twickenham, just 15 minutes walk from the stadium.

Weekend breakfast 9am

We like to start the day as we mean to go on. Which is why we only use the finest ingredients, like our free-range eggs from British farms, or smoked salmon, fresh from the smokehouse on Loch Fyne. Whatever takes your fancy, there's no better way to start your day.

LOCH FYNE®
SEAFOOD & GRILL

www.lochfyneseafoodandgrill.co.uk

PREVIEW OF THE
SEASON 2015-16

Key Players
selected by IAN ROBERTSON

ENGLAND

GEORGE FORD
Bath
Born: 16 March 1993
Height: 5ft 10ins Weight: 13st 3lbs
Fly half – 11 caps
1st cap v Wales 2014

TOM YOUNGS
Leicester
Born: 28 January 1987
Height: 5ft 9ins Weight: 16st
Hooker – 22 caps (+3 Lions)
1st cap v Fiji 2012

SCOTLAND

GREIG LAIDLAW
Gloucester
Born: 12 October 1985
Height: 5ft 9ins Weight: 12st 8lbs
Scrum half/fly half – 39 caps
1st cap v New Zealand 2010

RICHIE GRAY
Castres
Born: 24 August 1989
Height: 6ft 9ins Weight: 19st 11lbs
Lock – 44 caps (+1 Lions)
1st cap v France 2010

WALES

JAMIE ROBERTS
Harlequins
Born: 8 November 1986
Height: 6ft 4ins Weight: 17st 4lbs
Centre – 69 caps (+3 Lions)
1st cap v Scotland 2008

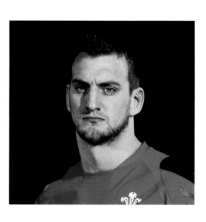

SAM WARBURTON
Cardiff Blues
Born: 5 October 1988
Height: 6ft 2ins Weight: 15st 8lbs
Back-row – 54 caps (+2 Lions)
1st cap v USA 2009

Six Nations Championship

2015-16

IRELAND

JOHNNY SEXTON
Leinster
Born: 11 July 1985
Height: 6ft 2ins Weight: 14st 6lbs
Fly half – 51 caps (+3 Lions)
1st cap v Fiji 2009

JAMIE HEASLIP
Leinster
Born: 15 December 1983
Height: 6ft 4ins Weight: 17st 4lbs
Back-row – 72 caps (+5 Lions)
1st cap v Pacific Islanders 2006

FRANCE

MORGAN PARRA
Clermont Auvergne
Born: 15 November 1988
Height: 5ft 11ins Weight: 12st
Scrum half – 59 caps
1st cap v Scotland 2008

THIERRY DUSAUTOIR
Toulouse
Born: 18 November 1981
Height: 6ft 2ins Weight: 16st 5lbs
Back-row – 75 caps
1st cap v Romania 2006

ITALY

LUKE MCLEAN
Treviso
Born: 29 June 1987
Height: 6ft 3ins Weight: 14st 11lbs
Utility back – 68 caps
1st cap v South Africa 2008

SERGIO PARISSE
Stade Français
Born: 12 September 1983
Height: 6ft 5ins Weight: 17st 4lbs
Back-row – 112 caps
1st cap v New Zealand 2002

Fixtures 2015-16

AUGUST 2015

Sat. 8th	WALES v IRELAND (w-u)
	AUSTRALIA v NZ (TRC/BC)
	SA v ARGENTINA (TRC)
Sat. 15th	ENGLAND v FRANCE (w-u)
	IRELAND v SCOTLAND (w-u)
	ARGENTINA v SA (w-u)
	NZ v AUSTRALIA (BC)
Sat. 22nd	FRANCE v ENGLAND (w-u)
	ITALY v SCOTLAND (w-u)
Sat. 29th	IRELAND v WALES (w-u)
	SCOTLAND v ITALY (w-u)
	BT Scottish Premiership (1)
	BT Scottish National Lges 1-3

SEPTEMBER 2015

Fri. 4th to	
Sun. 6th	Greene King IPA Championship
	Guinness PRO12 (1)
Sat. 5th	ENGLAND v IRELAND (w-u)
	WALES v ITALY (w-u)
	FRANCE v SCOTLAND (w-u)
	English National Leagues
	BT Scottish Premiership
	BT Scottish National Lges 1-3
	Welsh Principality Pr/ship (1)
	SSE Swalec Welsh Ch/ship
	SSE Swalec Welsh Nat Lges
Fri 11th and	
Sat. 12th	UB Irish Leagues
Fri. 11th to	
Sun. 13th	Guinness PRO12 (2)
Sat. 12th	English National Leagues
	BT Scottish Premiership
	BT Scottish National Lges 1-3
	Welsh Principality Pr/ship (2)
	SSE Swalec Welsh Ch/ship
	SSE Swalec Welsh Nat Lges
Sat. 12th and	
Sun. 13th	Greene King IPA Championship
Fri. 18th and	
Sat. 19th	UB Irish Leagues
Sat. 19th	English National Leagues
	BT Scottish Premiership
	BT Scottish National Lges
	Welsh Principality Pr/ship (3)
	SSE Swalec Welsh Ch/ship
	SSE Swalec Welsh Nat Lges
Sat. 19th and	
Sun. 20th	Greene King IPA Championship
Fri. 25th and	
Sat. 26th	UB Irish Leagues 1B, 2A & B
Sat. 26th	English National Leagues
	BT Scottish Premiership
	BT Scottish Cup (1)
	Welsh Principality Pr/ship (4)
	SSE Swalec Welsh Ch/ship
	SSE Swalec Bowl (1)

Sat. 26th and	
Sun. 27th	Greene King IPA Championship

OCTOBER 2015

Fri. 2nd to	
Sun. 4th	Guinness PRO12 (3)
Sat. 3rd	English National Leagues
	BT Scottish Premiership
	BT Scottish National Lges 1-3
	Welsh Principality Pr/ship (5)
	SSE Swalec Welsh Ch/ship
	SSE Swalec Welsh Nat Lges
	UB Irish Leagues
Sat. 3rd and	
Sun. 4th	Greene King IPA Championship
Fri. 9th	BT Scottish Premiership
Fri. 9th to	
Sun. 11th	Greene King IPA Championship
Sat. 10th	English National Leagues
	BT Scottish National League 1
	Welsh Principality Pr/ship (6)
	SSE Swalec Welsh Ch/ship
	SSE Swalec Welsh Nat Lges
	UB Irish Leagues 1B & 2A
Fri. 16th and	
Sat. 17th	Greene King IPA Championship
	UB Irish Leagues
Fri. 16th to	
Sun. 18th	Aviva English Premiership (1)
	Guinness PRO12 (4)
Sat. 17th	English National Leagues
	BT Scottish Premiership
	BT Scottish National Leagues
	Welsh Principality Pr/ship (7)
	SSE Swalec Welsh Ch/ship
	SSE Swalec Plate (1)
	SSE Swalec Bowl (2)
Fri. 23rd to	
Sun. 25th	Greene King IPA Championship
	Guinness PRO12 (5)
Sat. 24th	Aviva English Premiership (2)
	English National Leagues
	BT Scottish Premiership
	BT Scottish National Lges 1-3
	Welsh Principality Pr/ship (8)
	SSE Swalec Welsh Ch/ship
	SSE Swalec Welsh Nat Lges
	UB Irish League 2B
Fri. 30th and	
Sat. 31st	UB Irish Leagues 1A & B, 2B
Fri. 30th to	
Sun. 1 Nov.	Guinness PRO12 (6)
Sat. 31st	BT Scottish Premiership
	BT Scottish National Lges 1-3
	Welsh Principality Pr/ship (9)
Sat. 31st and	
Sun. 1st Nov.	Aviva English Premiership (3)

NOVEMBER 2015

Fri. 6th to	
Sun. 8th	Greene King IPA Championship
	Guinness PRO12 (7)
Sat. 7th	Aviva English Premiership (4)
	English National Leagues
	BT Scottish Premiership
	BT Scottish National Lges 1-3
	Welsh Principality Pr/ship (10)
	SSE Swalec Welsh Ch/ship
	SSE Swalec Welsh Nat Lges
	UB Irish Leagues
Thu.12th to	
Sun. 15th	European Champions Cup (1)
	European Challenge Cup (1)
Fri. 13th to	
Sun. 15th	British & Irish Cup (1)
Sat. 14th	English National Leagues
	BT Scottish Premiership
	BT Scottish National Lges 1-3
	SSE Swalec Welsh Ch/ship
	SSE Swalec Welsh Nat Lges
	Welsh Premier Challenge Cup
Thu. 19th to	
Sun. 22nd	European Champions Cup (2)
	European Challenge Cup (2)
Fri. 20th to	
Sun. 22nd	British & Irish Cup (2)
Sat. 21st	Barbarians v ARGENTINA
	(Twickenham – Killik Cup)
	English National Leagues
	BT Scottish Premiership
	BT Scottish National Lges 1-3
	SSE Swalec Welsh Ch/ship
	SSE Swalec Welsh Nat Lges
	Welsh Premier Challenge Cup
Mon. 23rd	Aviva 'A' League
Fri. 27th to	
Sun. 29th	Greene King IPA Championship
	Guinness PRO12 (8)
Sat. 28th	Aviva English Premiership (5)
	English National Leagues
	BT Scottish Premiership
	BT Scottish National Lges 1-3
	Welsh Principality Pr/ship (11)
	SSE Swalec Welsh Ch/ship
	SSE Swalec Welsh Nat Lges
	UB Irish Leagues 1A & B, 2A
Mon. 30th	Aviva 'A' League

DECEMBER 2015

Fri. 4th and	
Sat. 5th	HSBC 7s Series (Dubai)
Fri. 4th to	
Sun. 6th	Guinness PRO12 (9)
Sat. 5th	Greene King IPA Championship
	English National Leagues
	BT Scottish Premiership
	BT Scottish National Lges 1-3
	Welsh Principality Pr/ship (12)
	SSE Swalec Welsh Ch/ship
	SSE Swalec Welsh Nat Lges
	UB Irish Leagues 1A & B, 2B
Sat. 5th and	
Sun. 6th	Aviva English Premiership (6)
Thu. 10th	Oxford U v Cambridge U
	OU Women v CU Women
	(both Twickenham)
Thu. 10th to	
Sun. 13th	European Champions Cup (3)
	European Challenge Cup (3)
Fri. 11th to	
Sun. 13th	British & Irish Cup (3)
Sat. 12th	English National Leagues
	BT Scottish Premiership
	BT Scottish National Lges 1-3
	SSE Swalec Welsh Ch/ship
	Welsh Premier Challenge Cup
	SSE Swalec Welsh Plate (2)
	SSE Swalec Welsh Bowl (3)
	UB Irish Leagues 2A & B
Sat. 12th and	
Sun. 13th	HSBC 7s Series (Cape Town)
Thu. 17th to	
Sun. 20th	European Champions Cup (4)
	European Challenge Cup (4)
Fri. 18th to	
Sun. 20th	British & Irish Cup (4)
Sat. 19th	English National Leagues
	BT Scottish Premiership
	BT Scottish National Lges 1-3
	SSE Swalec Welsh Ch/ship
	SSE Swalec Welsh Nat Lges
	Welsh Premier Challenge Cup
Mon. 21st	Aviva 'A' League
Sat. 26th	Welsh Principality Pr/ship (13)
	SSE Swalec Welsh Ch/ship
Sat. 26th and	
Sun. 27th	Aviva English Premiership (7)
	Greene King IPA Championship
	Guinness PRO12 (10)
Mon. 28th	Aviva 'A' League

JANUARY 2016

Fri. 1st and	
Sat. 2nd	Greene King IPA Championship
Fri. 1st to	
Sun. 3rd	Guinness PRO12 (11)
Sat. 2nd	Aviva English Premiership (8)
	English National Leagues
	Welsh Principality Pr/ship (14)
	SSE Swalec Welsh Ch/ship
	SSE Swalec Welsh Nat Lges
	UB Irish Leagues 1A & B
Mon. 4th	Aviva 'A' League
Fri. 8th to	
Sun. 10th	Guinness PRO12 (12)
Sat. 9th	English National Leagues
	BT Scottish Premiership
	BT Scottish National Lges 1-3
	SSE Swalec Welsh Nat Lges
	SSE Swalec Cup (1)

	UB Irish Leagues 1A, 2A & B
Sat 9th and	
Sun. 10th	Aviva English Premiership (9)
Thu. 14th to	
Sun. 17th	European Champions Cup (5)
	European Challenge Cup (5)
Sat. 16th	English National Leagues
	BT Scottish Premiership
	BT Scottish National Lges 1-3
	SSE Swalec Welsh Ch/ship
	Welsh Premier Challenge Cup
	SSE Swalec Plate (3)
	SSE Swalec Bowl (4)
	UB Irish Leagues 2A & B
Sat. 16th and	
Sun. 17th	British & Irish Cup (5)
Thu. 21st to	
Sun. 24th	European Champions Cup (6)
	European Challenge Cup (6)
Sat. 23rd	English National Leagues
	BT Scottish National Leagues
	SSE Swalec Welsh Ch/ship
	SSE Swalec Welsh Nat Lges
	Welsh Premier Challenge Cup
	UB Irish Lges 1A & B, 2A & B
	British & Irish Cup (6)
Fri. 29th and	
Sat. 30th	UB Irish Lges 1A & B, 2A & B
Fri. 29th to	
Sun. 31st	Guinness PRO12 (13)
Sat. 30th	English National Leagues
	Welsh Principality Pr/ship (15)
	SSE Swalec Welsh Ch/ship
	SSE Swalec Welsh Nat Lges
Sat. 30th and	
Sun. 31st	HSBC 7s Series (Wellington)
	Aviva English Premiership (10)
	Greene King IPA Championship
	BT Scottish Cup (2)

FEBRUARY 2016

Fri. 5th and	
Sat. 6th	UB Irish Leagues
Sat. 6th	FRANCE v ITALY (14:25)
	SCOTLAND v ENGLAND (16:50)
	English National Leagues
	SSE Swalec Cup (2)
Sat. 6th and	
Sun. 7th	HSBC 7s Series (Sydney)
	Aviva English Premiership (11)
	Greene King IPA Championship
Sun. 7th	IRELAND v WALES (15:00)
Fri. 12th and	
Sat. 13th	Greene King IPA Championship
	Guinness PRO12 (14)
Sat. 13th	FRANCE v IRELAND (14:25)
	WALES v SCOTLAND (16:50)
	English National Leagues
	BT Scottish National Lges 1-3
	Welsh Principality Pr/ship (16)
Sat. 13th and	
Sun. 14th	Aviva English Premiership (12)

Sun. 14th	ITALY v ENGLAND (14:00)
Fri. 19th and	
Sat. 20th	UB Irish Leagues
Fri. 19th to	
Sun. 21st	Guinness PRO12 (15)
Sat. 20th	English National Leagues
	Welsh Principality Pr/ship (17)
	SSE Swalec Welsh Ch/ship
	SSE Swalec Welsh Nat Lges
Sat. 20th and	
Sun. 21st	Aviva English Premiership (13)
	BT Scottish Cup (3)
Fri. 26th	WALES v FRANCE (20:05)
Fri. 26th to	
Sun. 28th	Guinness PRO12 (16)
Sat. 27th	ITALY v SCOTLAND (14:25)
	ENGLAND v IRELAND (16:50)
	SSE Swalec Welsh Ch/ship
	SSE Swalec Cup QF
	SSE Swalec Plate (4)
	SSE Swalec Bowl (5)
	UB Irish Leagues 1A & B, 2B
Sat. 27th and	
Sun. 28th	Aviva English Premiership (14)
	Greene King IPA Championship

MARCH 2016

Fri. 4th and	
Sat. 5th	Aviva English Premiership (15)
Fri. 4th to	
Sun. 6th	HSBC 7s Series (Las Vegas)
	Greene King IPA Championship
	Guinness PRO12 (17)
Sat. 5th	English National Leagues
	BT Scottish National Lges 1-3
	BT Scottish Cup QF
	Welsh Principality Pr/ship (18)
	SSE Swalec Welsh Ch/ship
	SSE Swalec Welsh Nat Lges
	UB Irish Leagues
	*British & Irish Cup QF
Sat. 12th	IRELAND v ITALY (13:30)
	ENGLAND v WALES (16:00)
	Aviva English Premiership (16)
	BT Scottish National Lges 1-3
	Welsh Principality Pr/ship (19)
Sat. 12th and	
Sun. 13th	HSBC 7s Series (Vancouver)
Sun. 13th	SCOTLAND v FRANCE (15:00)
Wed. 16th	NatWest Schools' Cup Day
	(Twickenham)
Fri. 18th to	
Sun. 20th	*British & Irish Cup SF
Sat. 19th	WALES v ITALY (14:30)
	IRELAND v SCOTLAND (17:00)
	FRANCE v ENGLAND (20:00)
	English National Leagues
	SSE Swalec Plate QF
	SSE Swalec Bowl QF
Sat. 19th and	
Sun. 20th	Aviva English Premiership (17)
Wed. 23rd	BUCS Finals (Twickenham)

Fri. 25th and Sat. 26th	UB Irish Leagues 2A & B
Fri. 25th to Sun. 27th	Greene King IPA Championship Guinness PRO12 (18)
Sat. 26th	BT Scottish National Lges 1-3 BT Scottish Cup SF BT Scottish Shield SF BT Scottish Bowl SF Welsh Principality Pr/ship (20) SSE Swalec Welsh Ch/ship SSE Swalec Welsh Nat Lges
Sat. 26th and Sun. 27th	Aviva English Premiership (18)
Mon. 28th	Aviva 'A' League

APRIL 2016

Fri. 1st and Sat. 2nd	Greene King IPA Championship
Fri. 1st to Sun. 3rd	Guinness PRO12 (19)
Sat. 2nd	Aviva English Premiership (19) English National Leagues Welsh Principality Pr/ship (21) SSE Swalec Welsh Ch/ship SSE Swalec Welsh Nat Lges
Thu. 7th to Sun. 10th	European Champions Cup QF European Challenge Cup QF
Fri. 8th to Sun. 10th	HSBC 7s Series (Hong Kong)
Sat. 9th	SSE Swalec Welsh Ch/ship SSE Swalec Welsh Nat Lges **SSE Swalec Plate SF **SSE Swalec Bowl SF British & Irish Cup Final
Mon. 11th	Aviva 'A' League
Fri. 15th to Sun. 17th	Greene King IPA Championship Guinness PRO12 (20)
Sat. 16th	English National Leagues BT Scottish Cup Final BT Scottish Shield Final BT Scottish Bowl Final **SSE Swalec Cup SF UB Irish Leagues 1A & B
Sat. 16th and Sun. 17th	HSBC 7s Series (Singapore) Aviva English Premiership (20)
Thu. 21st to Sun. 24th	*European Champions Cup SF *European Challenge Cup SF
Sat. 23rd	St George's Day Game (Twickenham) Greene King IPA Championship English National Leagues Welsh Principality Pr/ship (22)
Mon. 25th	Aviva 'A' League SF
Fri. 29th to Sun. 1st May	Guinness PRO12 (21)
Sat. 30th	Greene King IPA Ch/ship SF

	English National Leagues English Nat Lges/Divisional Play-offs Army v Navy (Babcock Trophy) Combined Services U23 v Oxbridge U23 (both Twickenham)
Sat. 30th and Sun. 1st May	Aviva English Premiership (21)

MAY 2016

Mon. 2nd	Aviva 'A' League Final
Fri. 6th to Sun. 8th	Guinness PRO12 (22)
Sat. 7th	Aviva English Premiership (22) Greene King IPA Ch/ship SF English Nat Lges 1 & 2 Play-off RFU Intermediate Cup Final RFU Senior Vase Final RFU Junior Vase Final English National U20 Cup Final Welsh Principality Pr/ship SF
Fri. 13th and Sat. 14th	European Challenge Cup Final European Champions Cup Final (both Lyon, France)
Sat. 14th	Greene King IPA Ch/ship Final (1)
Sat. 14th and Sun. 15th	HSBC 7s Series (Paris)
Fri. 20th and Sat. 21st	*Aviva English Premiership SF
Fri. 20th to Sun. 22nd	*Guinness PRO12 SF
Sat. 21st and Sun. 22nd	HSBC 7s Series (London) Greene King IPA Ch/ship Final (2) Welsh Principality Pr/ship Final
Fri. 27th to Sun. 29th	*Guinness PRO12 Final
Sat. 28th	Aviva English Premiership Final
Sun. 29th	ENGLAND v TBC English Cty Ch/ship Final (Bill Beaumont Cup) English Cty Ch/ship Plate Final English Cty Ch/ship Shield Final

Key

(w-u) = RWC warm-up match
(TRC) = The Rugby Championship, successor
competition to the Tri-Nations
(BC) = Bledisloe Cup
* dates and times to be confirmed
** date and time of final to be confirmed